COOPERS ADJUTANTS . . . AND THE UNSUNG HEROICS AND DEEDS OF CLERKS IN GRAY!

A History of the Life and Times of General Samuel Cooper, AG

General Samuel Cooper

The Life and times of one of the grandest military administrators of all times . . . .

The Adjutant and Inspector General
Confederate War Department
(Northerner by birth—Southern by devotion)

COL CHARLES W. L. HALL, PH.D.

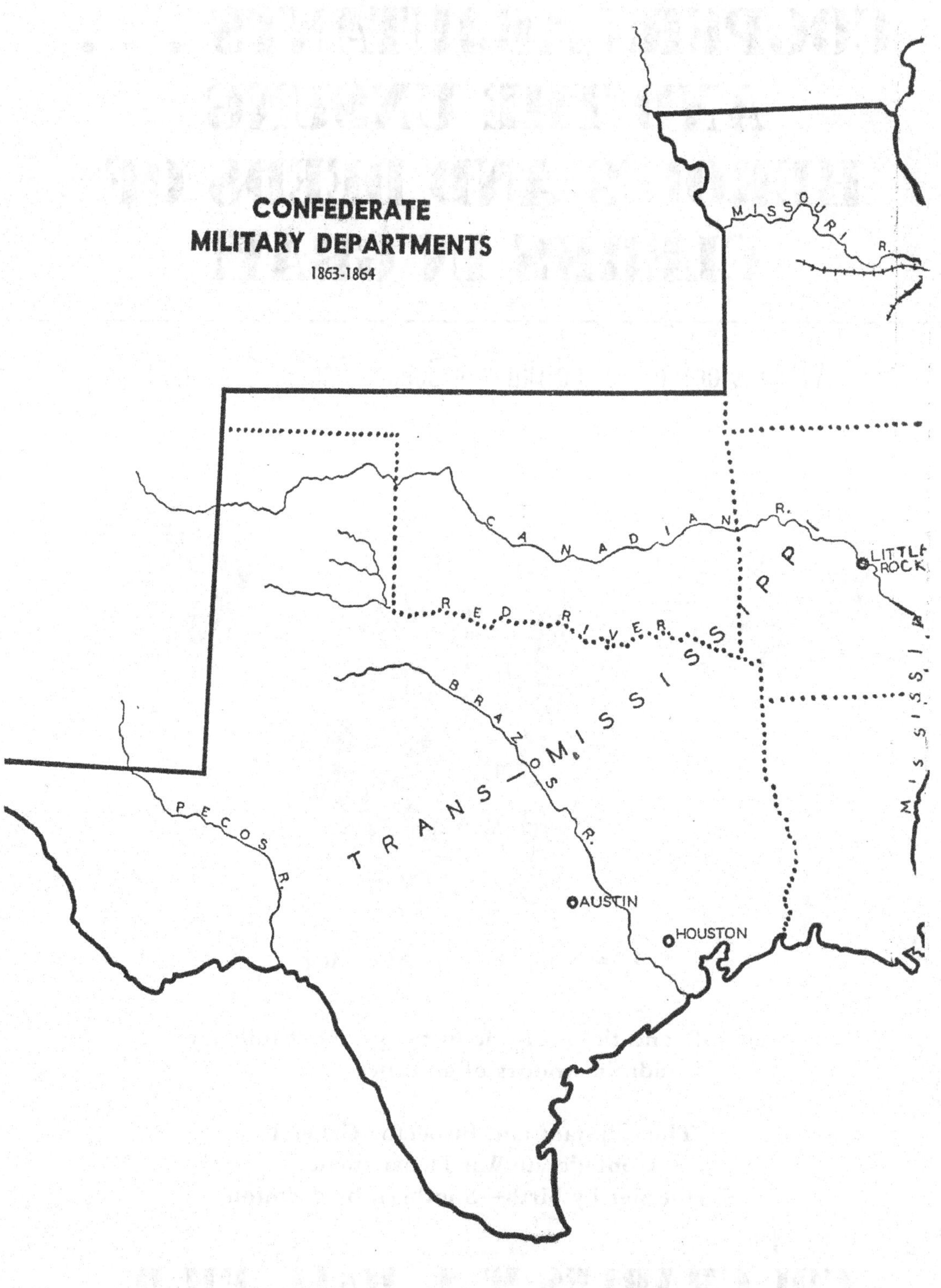
CONFEDERATE
MILITARY DEPARTMENTS
1863-1864
MISSOURI R.
CANADIAN R.
RED RIVER
BRAZOS R.
PECOS R.
TRANS-MISSISSIPPI
AUSTIN
HOUSTON

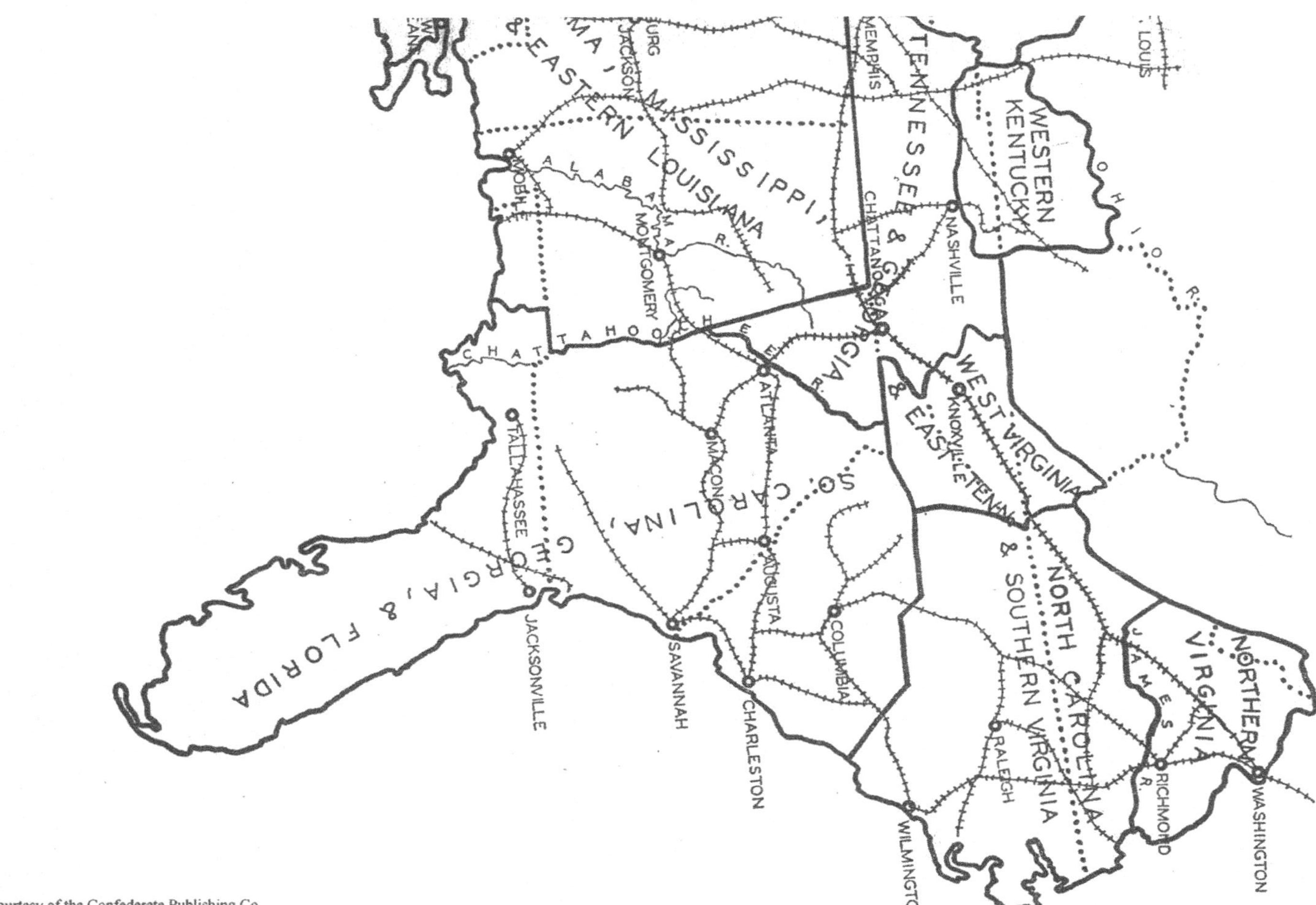

Courtesy of the Confederate Publishing Co.

M-1. The Confederate States of American, highlighting the Military Departments of the Confederate War Department theaters of war.

COOPERS ADJUTANTS . . . AND THE UNSUNG HEROICS AND DEEDS OF CLERKS IN GRAY!

A History of the Life and Times of General Samuel Cooper, AG

The Life and times of one of the grandest military administrators of all times . . . .

The Adjutant and Inspector General
Confederate War Department
(Northerner by birth—Southern by devotion)

COL CHARLES W. L. HALL, PH.D.

Order this book online at www.trafford.com
or email orders@trafford.com

Most Trafford titles are also available at major online book retailers.

Library of Congress Cataloging-in-Publication Data

Cooper, Samual., b. 1798 d. 1876.

Cooper's Adjutants, and the unsung heroics & deeds of Clerks in Gray: a history of the Confederate Adjutant & Inspector General 1861-1866: and the Civil War memories of the men of the Confederacy / complied and edited by COL Charles W.L. Hall,

p. cm.
Includes bibliographical references and index.

1. Confederate States of America. Army. Adjutant & Inspector General's Staff.
2. United States—History—Civil War, 1861-1865—War Department histories.
3. Virginia—History—Civil War, 1860-1865—War Department histories.
4. United States—History—Civil War, 1861-1865—Personal narratives, Confederate.
5. Virginia—History—Civil War, 1861-1865—Personal narratives.
6. Jones, J. B. b.—Diary.
7. Soldiers—Virginia—Richmond—Memors. I. Hall, Charles W.L., 1946—. II Titles.

E546.S58 973.7462' 00-00000
For Virginia, CSA: CIP
E341.S65 973.762'

British Library Cataloging in Publication Data Available

Printed in the United States of America.

ISBN: 978-1-4669-7872-0 (sc)
ISBN: 978-1-4669-7871-3 (e)

Trafford rev. 10/23/2013

www.trafford.com

North America & international
toll-free: 1 888 232 4444 (USA & Canada)
fax: 812 355 4082

THE LIFE AND TIMES
OF
GENERAL SAMUAL COOPER

A

Soldier

Adjutant and Inspector GENERAL

Courtesy of the generalcooper.com

General Samuel Cooper Fig. 1

Confederate Veteran.

PUBLISHED MONTHLY IN THE INTEREST OF CONFEDERATE VETERANS AND KINDRED TOPICS.

Entered at the post office at Nashville, Tenn., as second-class matter.
Contributors are requested to use only one side of the paper, and to abbreviate as much as practicable. These suggestions are important.
Where clippings are sent copy should be kept, as the VETERAN cannot undertake to return them. Advertising rates furnished on application
The date to a subscription is always given to the month *before* it ends. For instance, if the VETERAN is ordered to begin with January, the date on mail list will be December, and the subscriber is entitled to that number.

The *civil* war was too long ago to be called the *late* war, and when correspondents use that term "War between the States" will be substituted.
The terms "New South" and "lost cause" are objectionable to the VETERAN.

OFFICIALLY REPRESENTS:

UNITED CONFEDERATE VETERANS,
UNITED DAUGHTERS OF THE CONFEDERACY,
SONS OF VETERANS, AND OTHER ORGANIZATIONS,
CONFEDERATED SOUTHERN MEMORIAL ASSOCIATION.

The VETERAN is approved and indorsed officially by a larger and more elevated patronage, doubtless, than any other publication in existence.

Though men deserve, they may not win success;
The brave will honor the brave, vanquished none the less.

PRICE, $1.00 PER YEAR. SINGLE COPY, 10 CENTS. | VOL. XIV. NASHVILLE, TENN., FEBRUARY, 1906. NO. 2. | S. A. CUNNINGHAM, PROPRIETOR.

GEN. SAMUEL COOPER.

The least known of any official in the Confederate government, his rank and efficiency considered, was Samuel Cooper.

General Samuel Cooper was born either in Hackensack, N. J., or in New York State June 12, 1798. At the age of fifteen he entered the United States Military Academy at West Point, graduating in 1817, the period of study not being so long then as now—four years. He obtained the full rank of lieutenant at the age of seventeen years. He was aid-decamp to Gen. Macomb, the general in chief of the army, 1828-36. He was assistant adjutant general at army headquarters during the Florida War. For meritorious conduct relating to the Mexican War he was brevetted colonel on the staff, and in 1852 became the adjutant general of the United States army. He held this rank till 1861, save while serving temporarily as Secretary of War.

In March, 1861, he resigned his commission and went at once to Montgomery, Ala., reporting to President Jefferson Davis on March 15, and the next day was appointed by President Davis adjutant general of the Confederate States, standing at the head of the list of Confederate generals. That master mind for the skillful organization of an army arrived in Montgomery at the very moment of the demand, and he was evidently the best-prepared man in America for that particular work. Association between Gen. Cooper and Mr. Davis while the latter was Secretary of War doubtless caused them to know each other fully.

It is singular that one of the last official acts of Gen. Cooper as adjutant general of the United States was to sign an order of dismissal from the United States army of Brig. Gen. David E. Twiggs, who became a Confederate major general. That order bears date March 1, 1861, and Gen. Cooper's resignation was dated March 7.

The absence of historic data prevents the VETERAN from giving reasons why Gen. Cooper resigned from the United States army to take his chances with the Confederate government, but throughout that strenuous period there is no known record of even lukewarmness in his service. He resided after the war near Alexandria, Va., until his death, which occurred in December, 1876.

President Davis, in his "Rise and Fall of the Confederate Government," gives Gen. Cooper's birthplace as New York. He reports as the first officers to resign and enlist for the South Samuel Cooper, Albert Sidney Johnston, and R. E. Lee, and that "Samuel Cooper was the first of these to offer his services to the Confederacy at Montgomery. Having known him most favorably and intimately as adjutant general of the United States army when I was Secretary of War, the value of his services in the organization of a new army was considered so great that I invited him to the position of adjutant general of the Confederate army, which he accepted without a question as to relation, rank, or anything else. The highest grade then authorized by law was that of brigadier general, and that commission was bestowed upon him."

It is recorded that Gen. Cooper was promoted to the rank of general on August 31, 1861, and that he was throughout the ranking general of the armies of the Confederate States.

OFFICIAL REUNION ORDER.

In issuing General Order No. 38 from New Orleans, La., January 15, 1906, Adjt. Gen. Mickle states: "The sixteenth annual Reunion of the United Confederate Veterans will be held in the city of New Orleans, La., April 25-27, 1906, Wednesday, Thursday, Friday, respectively, those days having been named by our host as satisfactory. There are many reasons why the Reunion of 1906 should surpass any heretofore held. The city of New Orleans is geographically situated so as to be easily accessible to a large section of our Federation. It is near the great Trans-Mississippi Department, with its thousands of enthusiastic old soldiers, and the most populous divisions of the other departments are not distant. The longing of the gallant remnants of the Confederate armies to meet each other, which each year grows stronger, the peculiar character of the city with its innumerable attractions, its old-time streets, its antique buildings, its immense shipping with countless craft that float on the bosom of the 'great river,' the beauty and refinement of its women, the hospitality of its people, ever the most enthusiastic Confederates, the exceedingly low rate made by the railroads—all, coupled with the promise of its citizens—and with them promise is performance—that this gathering shall surpass all heretofore held, combine to make this a memorable Reunion. The General commanding, then, most earnestly urges all Camp officers to strive to have a large attendance from their Camps, that these aged men may once more have the pleasure of meeting their old comrades in arms. The General commanding with much pleasure announces, at the request of its most energetic President, Mrs. W. J. Behan, that the Confederated Southern Memorial Association will meet at the same time."

Fig. 2.

1st National "Stars & Bars"

War for Southern Independence

3rd National

Traditional
COLORS with HONORS

Symbols of the Confederate Army in the Field
"Army of North Virginia"

"Jackson's Corps" "The Battle Flag" "Longstreet's Corps"

Symbols of the Confederate Army in the Field
"Army of Tennessee"

"Polk's Corps" "The Battle Flag" "Hardee's Corps"

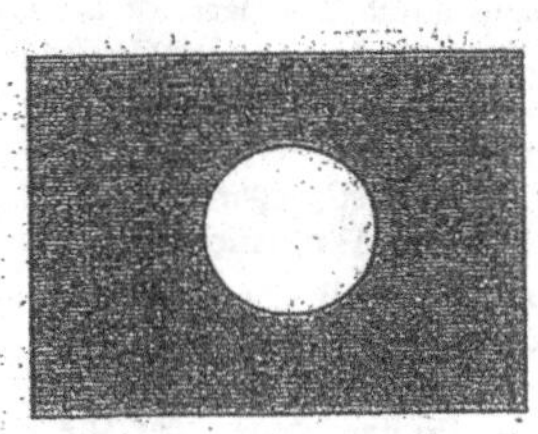

"Breckinridge's Corps"

1861 Montgomery, AL	1863 Richmond, VA	1865 (-) Danville, VA
Sec. War L.P. Walker★	Sec. War J.A. Seddon★	Sec. War J.C. Breckenridge

OFFICE OF THE ADJUTANT & INSPECTOR GENERAL CONFEDERATE STATES ARMY

Field and Staff—Headquarters, Provisional capitol, Montgomery, Alabama
General Samuel Cooper (16 May 61), Adjutant-Inspector General

Assistant Adjutant General—Executive Officer
Orderly Sergeant

Commissions & Promotions Branch
Lieutenant-Colonel Edward A. Palfrey ( )
Assistant Adjutant General

Transferors & Separations Branch
Lieutenant-Colonel John Withers ( )
Assistant Adjutant General

Recruiting & Instruction Branch
(Bureau of Conscription)
Brigadier General John S. Preston ( ) South Carolina
Assistant Adjutant General

Strength Reports Branch
Clerk

Orders & Files Management Branch
Clerk

Military Operations Branch
Clerk

Bureau of Exchange (POW)
Colonel Robert Ould ( ) Virginia
Signal Branch / Corps
Major William Norris ( )

Headquarters, Commandant Branch
Officer in Charge
Supply & Transportation Branch
NOC in charge
Local Details Branch
NCO in charge

Dedications

&

Memories . . . .

In preservation of my children's Southern heritage . . .

and,

the challenge of my cousin Dale Greenwell, in his successful writing of the 3rd Mississippi Infantry, C.S.A.;

In the memory of my dear friend, mentor, compatriot and scholar

The late

Major-General William D. McCain, US Army. Retired.
Adjutant-in-Chief, Sons of Confederate Veterans;

and

My fellow friends & compatriots of the

The Children of the Confederacy & the United Daughters of the Confederacy
Louisville, Jefferson County, Kentucky
1970-2010;

The Confederate Veterans, ladies and children
the of the South.

and

In the memory of our beloved

Confederacy . . . !

COOPERS' ADJUTANTS

The unsung Heroics and deeds

of

C L E R K S I N G R A Y!

The Life and Times of
General Samuel Cooper
A&IG
CSA

CONTENTS

[For "Register of Confederate War Department Officials and General Staff; "Partial Register of Assistant Adjutant General in Departments, Armies, Corps, Division, Brigade and Commands;" Partial Lists of Confederate regulations, directives, orders, documents, forms of the A&IG;" List of tables and illustrations" see Appendices.]

Manuscript Department
Library of UNC at Chapel Hill
"Southern Historical Collection"

INTRODUCTION

There are no more survivors of the Confederate War Department or its divisions & branches. Their heroic deeds and adventurous exploits have been buried in the archives and libraries of last resort, much like the "volunteers in gray" who were interned along the dusty roads and byways across the battlefields of the Southern Confederacy, a legacy paved in victories, defeats, and finally in surrender! They returned home beaten and wore on the outside, but victorious on the inside from a higher morale plain of satisfaction—knowing that they had given there very best, and yet, they had served honorable, but in their mind they remained un-surrendered in their cause.

I the author have been interested in the War for Southern Independence since I was a young child, that interest was reinforced by the excitement of the Centennial 1960-1965, and finally brought to fruitarian through my own family's genealogical research. My interest in the Confederate Adjutant General's Corps, was crystallized when the late President-Major General William D. McCain, University of Southern Mississippi, ask me to form a Son's of Confederate Veterans camp in Hattiesburg, Mississippi (a camp had not existed here since the 1950's).

At this time General McCain was serving also as the Adjutant-in-Chief, Son's of Confederate Veterans, headquartered at USM, and operated the Mississippi Division, Headquarters Camp #584 (of which I was a member in good standing since being credentialed in December 1972, while serving in the United States Army at Fort Ord, California).

I thought it a challenge and undertook to raise the Hattiesburg SCV Camp #1329. Some years later, having success with organizing this camp, I applied lessons learned upon returning to Louisville, Kentucky for a Master's program at the University of Louisville. I set about organizing the Louisville SCV Camp #1342, "the Orphan Brigade" (the Second Kentucky Infantry Regiment of Volunteers), of the Kentucky Division, Department of the Army of Tennessee SCV. Prior to the actual chartering of the Camp, I had been aware of this unit's history as a youth and heard the local folklore of these men.

During my participation in the Centennial reenactments—I discovered that Kentucky and Missouri were among the areas in the South where in was known that "brother fought brother and families were split over the war!" While researching the Confederate Archives at the Folsom Club and U of L, and later the Kentucky State Archives & History in Frankfort, I further discovered that the south had nearly nothing in terms of resources and facilities to raise and support a large standing army for a long drawn out war. That Samual Cooper was the miracle man in creating a

Confederate military bureaucracy from virtually nothing accept his own professional military experience and the willingness of 13 Confederate States to voluntarily provide there limited assets for use.

As a member of the United States Army, Adjutant General's Corps from 1963 to 1994, I had the opportunity to observe the corps in peacetime and war time through three major conflicts. I have as well, served in most AG positions, and from bottom to top in the staff's shadow chain of command to Headquarters, Department of the Army.

To further augment my knowledge of the Confederate AG, I have worked in Civil War Reenactments and displays of Living History's from 1980-1992; serving as an stereotypical Confederate Army Assistant Adjutant General officer (AAG), in the Army of Tennessee, CSA in both uniform, equipment, and role operations circa 1863.

During early 1861, the Kentucky State Legislature and Missouri State Legislature passed an act, for the expansion of the Kentucky and Missouri State Guards and other military forces. Early recruitment was under taken by the state guard, state militia and patriotic citizens. Southern sympathizers undertook to organize a new regiment for the Confederacy.

Upon the initial organization of the regiment in camp, and the completion of area recruitment of nearly 1,050 men to fulfill personnel requirements of 10 infantry companies and regimental headquarters field & staff; training of the regiment could begin in earnest.

Upon the receipt of orders, the men and officers of the Confederate States Army were jubilant and full of anticipation of the battle glory's to come—when they would finally met the "dam Yankee" on the field of contest and honor! They knew there patriotism and fidelity would lead to a triumph victory.

During 1861 and early 1862, the war was well under way in Kentucky, Virginia, Missouri, Tennessee, and Louisiana. As of this time, the Confederacy had not as yet under taken any major campaign, the present emphasis was a war plan based on defensive posture—in other words waging a border war, buying time to muster available men and material from the interior states. The War and Naval Departments of the Confederacy needed time to develop war industries and procure all available arms and munitions from abroad. During this initial period they became aware that Gulf and Atlantic coastlines were relatively free of conquest, and the sea lanes were wide open for trade.

Northern newspapers and local intelligence reported Union forces gathering along the Ohio River, and they were engaged in collecting river craft—it became apparent that there first objective would be to breach the Confederacy's defensive line along the Tennessee and Cumberland Rivers making Fort Henry, and Fort Donelson prime targets for assault. It was evident that the union war effort was pushing westward from the mountains of Western Virginia, to central Kentucky, and towards the Mississippi.

By Mid-February 1862, union forces were on the move, first they attacked with the support of Gunboats and overwhelmed the small garrison at Fort Henry on the Tennessee River—feeling fearless they immediately headed for Fort Donelson at Dover. The defensive line was under the overall command of General Albert S. Johnston in headquartered at Nashville.

The major operation for fall of 1862: A contest for the Border States. The major Confederate strategy was a three prong invasion of Central-Eastern Kentucky to secure Kentucky's admission to the Confederacy—in pronouncement of the states election to secede, and installation of its new Confederate Governor elect, at the state capitol in Frankfort.

COL Charles W. L. Hall, PhD.
United States Army, AGC, Retired
Confederate Historian

PART ONE

"There is nothing like
Army life . . . . !"

THE AMERICAN WAY OF WAR

CHAPTER I

The Cooper Legacy and Early childhood on the Atlantic Seaboard

Sketch of the Late General S. Cooper
By General Fitzhugh Lee

Students of military history cannot fail to be impressed, when war is *au fait accompli*, with the great advantage possessed by those nations who have justly placed a value upon system and organization in the preparation of their armies.

The military genius implanted by nature in a Caesar, a Hannibal, a Wellington, or a Napoleon, might never have burst forth with such overpowering light as to dazzle with its rays a wondering world, had not the human tools with which they worked been so formed, so fashioned, as to be perfectly flexible when placed in their hands by some almost hidden but powerful agent, who, grasping the subject with a master's mind, adapted the various departments of war in such a way as to work harmoniously together, and to be most effective, Strategy and grand tactics are indeed a powerful machine, but to be used to full working strength, requires an exact adjustment of all component parts.

To "set a squadron in the field," there must be arms, subsistence stores, transportation and shelters, clothing and medical supplies. The quartermaster's commissary, ordnance and medical departments, though separate and distinct in their several spheres, must be made comfortable with each others, with scrupulous care, by the constitutional commander-in-chief and his war secretary; and their chief counselor is the soldier at the head of the adjutant-general's department, through whom all official orders are promulgated. An efficient executive leader in that department is felt from an army corps to a corporal's guard.

Chronicles of the important events in the rise and fall of nations are filled with instructive instances that might be drawn upon in illustration of this fact, whilst the pages of history, where results are summed up and explanatory reasons given to them, abound in examples. To keep this paper within proper limits, I shall only briefly refer to one, viz.: The Franco-Prussian war of 1870.

The French Emperor, it is recollected, declared war because the King of Prussia would not promise that the head of the Catholic branch of the royal family, Prince Leopold of Hohenzollern, should never again be a candidate for the throne of Spain. The great and unquestioned ability of Louis Napoleon was deemed evidence that all things were duly weighed, and that his organization and preparations were at least complete. The French army numbered some 350,000 trained soldiers. The population of France was 38,067,064 in relationship to which, says their president of the legislative body to the Emperor, as he was about to depart for the frontier: "Behind you, behind our army accustomed to carry the noble flag of France, stands the whole nation, ready to recruit it."

On the other side, Prussia had a population of some twenty-four millions, or, including the North German Confederation (of which she is a part) of some thirty millions. Her standing army numbered less than 400,000. To what was due, then, the astounding results of the conquest, for the world was prepared for a gigantic and not unequal combat? Why, in the short space of six months, do we witness a Sedan, with capitulation by McMahon of 90,000 men? A Metz, with a surrender of nearly 200,000 by Bazaine? A Strasburg, giving up 17,000 soldiers? And speedily the fall of Paris, with a war indemnity to be paid the victors of five millions of francs? Why such a series of victories of Germany, such inglorious defeats of France? Why such a rapid fall of the curtain upon such a striking tableau vivant? We trace it to the weakness and inefficiency of the military organization of France, and to the wisdom of the system which gave the preponderating power of the reserves to Germany-the marvelous comprehensive military method that beings, at the tap of the drum, thousands of drilled, disciplined men to the support of the main body, as opposed to conscription or enlistment of raw levies from the population at large.

King William and Von Moltke strongly felt the hand of Shamhorst, who undertook the reorganization of the military resources of Prussia after Jena in 1806-an honor in our war which leaders as Albert Sydney Johnson, Lee. Johnston, Beauregard and Jackson must share a Cooper., whose judgment and masterly ability quietly plan, arrange and direct the machinery which is to put in motion by the brilliant army chieftains, such a I have mentioned, that wins success.

General Samuel Cooper possessed an inheritable right to his enviable eminence.

From Dorsetshire, England, his great grandfather came, and settled in Massachusetts. This paternal ancestor had three sons-John, the grandfather of General Cooper, Samuel and William. Samuel was President of Harvard University during the Revolutionary war, and was proscribed by General Gage of the British army, and a reward offered for his head. The son of John, also called Samuel, was the father of General Cooper. At eighteen years old, we find him at Lexington, forming one of seventy men that "assembled in front of the meeting-house," to whom Major Pitcairn, commanding the British advance, called out "disperse, you rebels, throw down your arms and disperse," on the morning of the 19th April 1775. Early manifesting such a heroic spirit, it was not surprising that he should have been found upon the night of 16th June marching with Prescott, and working all night upon a redoubt on Breed's Hill (mistaken for Bunker Hill, in the darkness of the night), and obeying sturdy old Putnam's orders on the morning of the 17th, not to fire "till they could see the whites of the eyes of the British."

He afterwards served with distinction in Knox's regiment of artillery, and upon his tombstone appears the following inscription:

> "Sacred to the memory of Major Samuel Cooper of the Revolutionary Army, who in the first onset struck for liberty.
>
> He fought at Lexington, Bunker Hill, Brandywine, Monmouth, Germantown, and on other sanguinary fields, and continued to wield the sword in defense of his country until victory crowned her arms."

At the close of the Revolutionary War, Major Cooper married Miss Mary Horton, of Dutchess County, New York. Two sons and six daughters were born from this marriage. George and Samuel (the subject of this memoir) were the sons. The former graduated at West Point, but afterwards went into the navy.

Adjutant-General Cooper was born in 1798, at Hackensack on the Judson river, at the family seat of his maternal ancestors. He entered the United States Military Academy at West Point when on fifteen years old.

(The following is retyped from the Southern Historical Society Papers., Volume III, January to June 1877, published in Richmond, VA by Rev. J. William Jones, D.D., Secretary Southern Historical Society. Pages 269-274.

And research of General Cooper's website receiving copies of E. Rowland Dawson's research paper.)

CHAPTER II

Cadet Samuel Cooper and his West Point Years

CADET SAMUEL COOPER
West Point, United States Military Academy

The young Samuel grew-up in a rural country setting with his family home at Hackensack village, along the river Judson. His life like most children was probably spent in doing household chores and day dreaming about being a warrior in the French & Indian War, or as a soldier fighting with General George Washington in the Revolutionary War (his father's war).

His father, Major Samuel Cooper, was a Revolutionary War hero in his own right, but had died about the time of his birth in June 12, 1798; his mother Mary was frail, very nurturing and protective; he had an older brother who was the man of the house and worked to earn a living for the family.

Samuel's personal development was overseen by the strict relatives of his mothers' side (of Boston, Mass.). His academic studies were under a tutor and his religious training in the Episcopal faith by the local church pastor. It seems he was a quick learner and steadfast with his (3R) studies. Apparently, Samuel had always been like his mother, gentle, soft spoken, and on the quiet side.

Samuel had always looked up to his fathers' image and his older brother as role models and wished to emulate them in life. Eventually, his older brother was nominated and admitted to West Point on the basis of his father's war record.

At the age of 14, Samuel wished to follow his brother into the military. With the blessing of his mother and the help of her family, young Samuel was nominated by there New York Congressman, and was admitted to West Point, United States Military Academy starting with the class of 1815 as plebe number 156. He fit in almost immediately. (All of Cooper's studies and activities occurred, with the backdrop of the War of 1812-1815).

(See Appendices) 2, 3, 4

Cadet Samuel Cooper came to the academy with the desired qualities of having good manners and decorum, always a gentleman, spoke softly, studied hard, paid close attention to detail, had a photographic memory, and excelled at reading and penmanship. Cooper began his military training with great excitement and expectations.

The Superintendent of West Point was a Brigadier General Joseph G. Swift (1812-1814), at the time of Cadet Cooper's admission. Cooper's academic and military instruction would be for the duration of two years, 1813-1815. During this time there must have been a great deal of discussion of the War of 1812, the defeats, the victories and the resulting treaties (especially, as it was reported in the early newspapers of the time). The first year's instruction, empathize the academics and basic military arts; the second year's instruction was much more technical: dealing with the scientific applications of Cavalry, Artillery and Engineering (the final result of this year would lead to there selected career path). Cadet Cooper's student records did not survive, but it is reasonable to expect that he never received and serious "demerits!" Apparently, he scored highest in his studies of "Artillery Tactics."

It is felt that he was a serious student (and today would have been called a Bookworm?!) On one final note of academy life, at social occasions, he was impeccable in social edicate and dancing, and all about "spite and polish (pomp & ceremonies)"!

In May 1815, he graduated 35th out of a class of 40. He received a regular army commission as a Brevetted 2nd Lieutenant in the Light Artillery, and was duly assigned to the First Artillery Regiment, Continental Army, and stationed at several New England garrison posts until 1818. 3, 4

New York 7th June 1813

I have the honor to acknowledge the receipt of your favour of the 25th ulto which came to hand on the 5th inst. covering my appointment as a Cadet in the Military Academy at West Point. It is with Pleasing Sensations accept it and beg leave to tender you my sincere acknowledgements for the honor conferred and at the same time to assure you it shall ever be my ambition to acquire a knowledge of my duty and prepare myself for the Service of my country

I have the Honor to be Sir very respectfully your Obedt Hble Servt

Saml Cooper Junr

The Honble Secretary at War

Courtesy of the USMA West Point

Fig. 4. Cooper's West Point Appointment Letter, 1813

CHAPTER III

The Davis War Department under the Pierce Administration

Fig .5. U.S. Secretary of War the Honorable Jefferson Davis, 1853

Courtesy of the Confederate Publishing Co.

The Davis War Department and Adjutant General Cooper's Office

In July 1838, Major Cooper as the assistant Adjutant-General at the U.S. War Department in Washington, DC, began his long career in senior military administration during the Martin Van Buren presidency (1837-1841). His legacy would be the opening and exploration of the western territories of a very young American nation. The Indian conflicts of the Northwestern and Southeastern regions were fermenting and would be soon coming to a close; bring down the "buckskin curtain" down blocking off the western lands. 4

In 1841, the Polk presidency (1841-1849) began with the first major military Indian Campaign against the Southeastern tribes, chiefly the Seminoles of Florida, as this would be his opportunity to serve in a multi-staffing environment as Chief of Staff of General Wool's headquarters. These operations came to a successful close in April 1842, thereby securing this part of the southern frontier. (Later, General Jackson undertook a similar successful campaign against the creeks). 4

Cooper retuned to his peacetime duties as the A.A.G. in Washington, Following the Texas declaration of 1846, soon thereafter the War Department would be making preparation to support Texas and fight the Mexican war. This was the first large scale military operation, since the Revolutionary war. A huge task was placed upon the Adjutant-General's Office to create two field armies (in recruiting, training, equipping and arming); and then sending them more than 2,000 miles away to fight a war against another foreign army, on its home turf. The American armies were victorious and Mexico was defeated, surrendering all of its western lands to the Pacific Ocean. Cooper's great efficiency in these preparations earned him praise and promotions to Lieutenant-Colonel in 1847, and Colonel in 1848. 4

Now sitting in the Adjutant-General's chair he would be a serving under the Zackary Taylor presidency (1849-1850). Shortly, thereafter, the Fillmore presidency (1850-1853) would take office, upon each succeeding presidency the western horizon grew wider, and the wagon trains continued to grow heading Northwest, West and Southwest, all needing army protection and support through a chain of fortifications, though the army was small—it under took the challenge. (In another 30 years the U.S. Army would conqueror the western plains). 4

With the advent of 1853, ushering in the Pierce presidency (1853-1857) and the Davis War Department, many changes would be on the move, permitting the modernization (especially in weapons) of the U.S. military forces to be undertaken. Jefferson Davis, the new secretary of war, had been a militia Colonel from Mississippi during the Mexican war, and later a U.S. Senator. The major political theme being—"opening the western lands" (as in a policy of "manifested destiny"), and complicated by the souring of north-south relations, as in the "Missouri Compromise of 1850!" Not only did the Davis War Department had to explore trails, build forts and maintain an ever increasingly long supply chain (communications, transportation, and food stuffs), but it had also to enforce law and order on the frontiers. 4

This put pressure on Cooper's Adjutant Office to expand the force, find adequate leadership, and recruit sufficient manpower to maintain our over-extended defense structure. Interestingly enough, Major Robert E. Lee would become the Superintendent of the U.S. Military Academy during this period. Jefferson Davis and the Pierce Administration wanted to promote the westward expansion of the railways toward the Pacific—and to connect overland with California. One of Davis' major projects was to send organized army engineer companies out west to discovery through surveying the best routes for the proposed railways. He strengthened coastal defenses. Another interesting scheme was to introduce Camels into the western deserts for possible use of the army. Davis was a very keen administrator himself. 4

Following the Pierce Administration, Davis was reelected to his U.S. Senate seat. 1857 witnessed greater fears of coming strife between the northern and southern sections of the country. So the Buchanan presidency (1857-1861) came in the under the gun, while trying to be neutral on the sectional disputes. Most men in uniform were debating the issues, and most southern states were expanding their state militia's and in controversy over possible secession. It had been said, that from the beginning, Adjutant-General Cooper and the Commander-in-Chief Winfield Scott had a personality clash. In the early 1850's, General Scott would send Colonel Cooper out west to inspect military installations and operations for extended periods for a peace of mind. 4

The political campaigns and elections of 1860 brought the north-south issues to the forefront and breaking point, the nation was dividing and so to was its military leaders.

Adjutant-General Cooper's last official act was to accept the resignation of Colonel David W. Twiggs from the U.S. Army in Texas dated March 1, 1861. Shortly, thereafter Colonel Samuel Cooper himself submitted his resignation from the U.S. Army dated March 7, 1861. Cooper ended his U.S. military career of nearly 46 years of loyal and faithful service at the age of 63. 4, 5

CHAPTER IV

Colonel Cooper as the Adjutant General in Washington, D.C.

Courtesy of the National Archives

Fig. 6. U.S. Adjutant General Samuel Cooper, 1835-1861

The Regular Army Career of Samuel Cooper A short sketch of as Compiled by George Alexander Cooper III

Adjutant-General Samuel Cooper, CSA was born on 12 June 1798, at Hackensack on the Judson river, at the family seat of his maternal ancestors, the Horton's. Growing up in rural New York, Dutchess county from 1798 to 1813, his early learning accomplished in a local Christian academy.

Age the age of 15, on May 25, 1813, Samuel entered the United States Military Academy, West Point, White Plains, New York as a Plebe. His term of service would be only two years, first year in academics and his second years in military arts. He graduated on December 10, 1815, thirty-sixth in his class of forty, being granted an army commission as a Lieutenant of light artillery of the Continental Army.

Probably around 1821 was promoted to First Lieutenant in the Third artillery. In 1824 was transferred to the Forth. From 1828 to 1836 he served as the aid-de-camp to Major-General Alexander Macomb, then commanding the American army, and was promoted to the rank of Captain on 11th June 1836.

Upon the 7th July, 1838, he first entered the U.S. War Department as an Assistant Adjutant and Inspector General in the rank of Major. During the Expeditions of the Seminoles Florida Indian war from 1841-42, he served as chief of staff to General Worth, and was in the action of Pila-Kil-Kaha on the 19th April 1842.

In 1847 was promoted to the rank of Lieutenant-Colonel, A.I.G. 1848 he was brevetted Colonel for meritorious conduct in the prosecution of his duties in connection with the Mexican war, and finally on 15th July 1852, was appointed the Adjutant and Inspector General of the United States Army in Washington, D.C.; General Winfield Scott being then its Commander-in-Chief.

Whilst in the United States Army during 1836, a time of peace, he wrote the first *Concise System of Instructions and Regulations for the Militia and Volunteers of the United States* (also known as "Tactics for the Militia"), a book at one time in almost universal use among the volunteer soldiery, and later revised and published as "Cooper's Tactics."

In 1827 at the age of 29, General Cooper (then Lieutenant) married Sarah Maria Mason, a daughter of General John Mason of Clermont, Fairfax, Virginia.

Sarah's grandfather was George Mason of Gunston, to whose memory the constitution of Virginia and her bill of rights are lasting monuments. George Mason was the author of the Virginia Declaration of Rights of 1776, and one of the three delegates to the Constitutional Convention of 1787 who would not sign the final draft.

Sarah's sister, Ann Maria Mason nicknamed "Nannie", was the mother of General Fitzhugh Lee whose father, Sidney Smith Lee, was the brother of General Robert

E. Lee, Sarah's brother the Hon. James Murray Mason was a member of the Virginia House of Representatives in 1837 and a Senator of Virginia in 1847.

Living in Washington, DC, Samuel spent his spare moments with his family at Cameron, Fairfax County, Virginia, and their estate near Alexandria. He and his family were friends of Robert E. Lee at nearby Arlington in the decade before the Civil War. From all indications, Sarah and Samuel were the parents of three children. One son who was also known as Samuel and one daughter known as Virginia (Jenny) and one daughter known as Maria, who died at a young age while giving birth.

The family connections of his wife Sarah, together with a close friendship with Jefferson Davis, which had grown when the latter was secretary of war, had made him wholly Southern in his feelings and sympathies. This was in spite of his Northern birth and ancestry.

At the outbreak of the Civil War, Samuel Cooper resigned his commission as Colonel, A&IG in the U.S. Army on March 7, 1861 at the age of 63.

He immediately traveled to Montgomery, Alabama by train and offered his service to the newly forming Confederacy. President Jefferson Davis at once offered him the position of Adjutant and Inspector General of the Confederate States Army with the rank of Brigadier-General. Shortly thereafter, the Confederate Congress approved of his appointment to the rank of the first and full general on 31st August 1861. He would be senior ranking officer of the Confederate Army throughout the war, reporting only to President Jefferson Davis. In Davis' memories the Rise and Fall of the Confederate Government, he reports that Samuel Cooper was the first officer to resign and enlisted for the South's defense.

(The research is the result of General Cooper's Website contributed to by G. A. Cooper III).

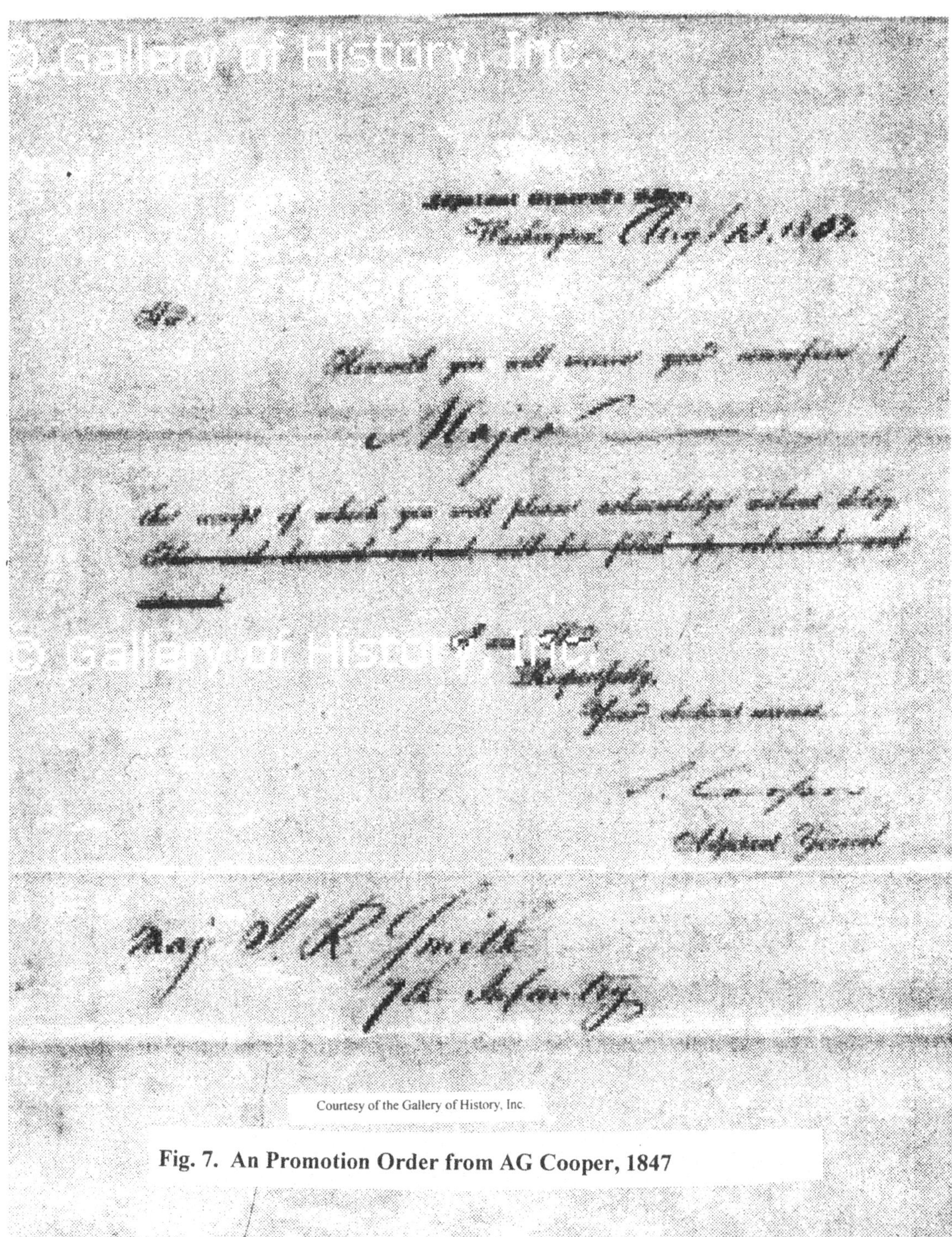

Adjutant General's Office,
Washington, Aug [illegible], 1847.

Sir:

Herewith you will receive your commission of

Major

the receipt of which you will please acknowledge without delay.
~~[illegible]~~

I am Sir,
Respectfully,
Your obedient servant,

[illegible]
Adjutant General

Maj. [illegible] R. Smith
7th Infantry

Courtesy of the Gallery of History, Inc.

Fig. 7. An Promotion Order from AG Cooper, 1847

PART TWO

"Hurrah for Dixie . . . . !"

THE SOUTH MOBILIZES FOR WAR

Courtesy of the National Archives

ISBN 0-86526-006-0(Volume I)
ISBN 0-86526-005-2 (Set)

Fig. 8. Confederate Recruiting Poster, 1861

CHAPTER V

Residing in the Confederate Capitols of Montgomery and Richmond

THE OLD MECHANICS' INSTITUTE.
(Used by the Confederates as the War Department; Destroyed in the Fire of Evacuati[illegible] Day.)

Courtesy of the Museum of the Confederacy

BRIGADIER GENERAL SAMUEL COOPER, CSA.

"The Confederate Capitols and War Department in 1861-1862"

The shift of Government from Montgomery, Alabama to Richmond, Virginia, is somewhat described in a diary maintained by a Mr. John B. Jones a principle clerk in the new war department. Jones made the following entries:

"May 15th (1861)—In the afternoon I walked to the capitol, a fine structure with massive columns, on a beautiful elevation, where I delivered several letters to the Virginia delegation in congress. They were exceedingly kind to me, and proffered their services very freely.

"May 16th—Met John Tyler, Jr., today who, with his native cordiality, proffered his services with zeal and earnestness. He introduced me at once to Hon. L. P. Walker, the 1st Secretary of War, and insisted upon presenting me to the President the next day. (Major Tyler had just been commissioned in the army, and detailed to assist the Hon. Walker in his correspondence). This is the same day, Colonel Samuel Cooper began his new job as the Adjutant and Inspector General of the Confederate army (later in August to be confirmed as a full general), also at the Exchange Hotel.

Apparently, according to Mr. Jones, he found the War Department offices located in the Exchange Hotel on the second floor, he further described the hotel thus: "the entrance to the bar, reading-room, etc. is by a flight of stairs from the street to the second story, with stores underneath. Here there is an incessant influx of strangers coming from all directions on business with the new government. But the prevalent belief is that the government itself will soon move to Richmond. The building here will be insufficient in magnitude for the transaction of the rapidly increasing business.

"On May 17th, after meeting the President, and on May 19th he (Jones) was employed by the Hon. Walker as a principle assistant with Major Tyler and immediately installed in the Secretary's office, with a temporary wage of $1,000-1,200 a month. Jones described is new duties thus: In was his duty to open and read the letters, noting briefly their contents on the back. The Secretary would then indicate in pencil marks the answer to be written, which the major and I prepared.

These were signed by the Secretary, copied in another room, and mailed. (I was happy in the discharge of these duties, and work assiduously day and night).

Mr. Jones then described his the trip to Richmond by train, thus: "The South is our only home—we have been only temporary sojourners elsewhere." May 29th and May 30th—He continues, "The remainder of the journey was without interest, until we arrived at Wytheville, Va., where it was discovered Gen. Floyd was in the cars. He was called out and made a speech in vindication of his conduct at Washington, as

Secretary of War, wherein he had caused the transfer of arms, etc. from the North to the South. He was then organizing a brigade in the field, having been commissioned a Brigadier General by President Davis.

May 31st—"I arrived in Richmond about 1 o'clock P.M. The meeting with my family was a joyful scene. All were well! I lost no time in securing rooms for the department in the new customs-house. Mr. Giles had been employed in this business by the Congressional Committee, and I found him every way accommodating. I succeeded without difficulty in convincing him that the War Department was the most important one, and hence entitled to the first choice of rooms. I therefore selected the entire suites on both sides of the hall on the lower floor. The Treasury, the Executive office, Cabinet chamber, and the Department of Justice and the Navy were located on the above floor. This arrangement, however, was understood to be but a temporary one; Mechanics Hall was leased for future purposes; and I consulted on the plan of converting it into suites of offices.

June 1st—"In the absence of the Secretary, I arranged the furniture as well as I could, and took possession of the five offices I had selected. But, no business, of course, could be done before his arrival. Yet, an immense mass of business was accumulating—letters by the hundreds were demanding attention.

"And I soon found, as the Secretaries came in, that some dissatisfaction was likely to grow out of the appropriation by the Secretary of War of the best offices. Mr. Toombs said the "war office" might do in any ordinary building; but Treasury should appropriately occupy the custom-house, which was fire proof. For his own department, he said he should be satisfied with a room or two anywhere. But my arrangement was not countermanded by the President, to whom I referred all objectors. His decision was final—and he did not decide against it. I have given him excellent quarters; and I knew he was in the habit of having frequent interviews both with the Secretary of War (Walker) and the Adjutant General (Cooper), and this would be inconvenient if they were in different buildings.

A Mr. W.C. Corsan gave an excellent report on the "Status of the Nation:" He began by saying, "Richmond is the safest, place in the Confederacy, and Southerner people know it well. When I was there, it was a very busy place. Its streets and hotels were literally crammed with soldiers, officers, and civilians, of all ranks, connected with Government business. Trains of quartermasters' wagons, bodies of Federal prisoners, ambulances with sick and wounded, mounted aides-de-camp, or masses of determined, though rough-looking Confederate troops, trailed through the streets incessantly.

"Many of the Government officers were in and around Bank Street, on the south side of the Capitol Square—once a quiet, retired locality, which never dreamed of ever being the scene of such turmoil and anxiety as it now is. The Mechanics' Institution, located on 9th Street, between Main and Franklin Streets, which faces down Bank

Street, a substantially built, but small and modest, brick edifice, never thoroughly finished inside, has been taken for the accommodations of the war, naval and other departments. (In fact, the building was home to War Department; lighthouse bureau of the Treasury; superintendent of government printing; commandant of the Confederate States Marine Corps; the ordnance, and the adjutant & inspector general's office).

"Inside Mechanics' Hall, were small, plain, unfurnished rooms, whose virgin walls never knew paper or whitewash, on whose woodwork no extravagant painter ever exhibited his skill, whose floors are innocent of carpet or any other covering, a small staff of civil, intelligent clerks, little common desks, with a very small show of stationery, dispatch with marvelous celerity all the multifarious business connected with the administration of an army of half million men, at least.

"The Secretary of War occupied what was once, I suppose, a Committee-room, rather better furnished, with which his clerk's office communicated, the door guard only by a lad. In and out of the door streamed, for six hours daily, all sorts of people, on all kinds of business, the most trivial and patent, or the most momentous and delicate. Those who had to wait their turn lounged about, smoking, chewing, laughing, and talking. And bullying the poor lad who kept the door of the temple of Janus. In one corner of the noisy, crowded room sat Judge John A. Campbell (assistant secretary of war) and perhaps a brigadier-general whose name whose name is a household word, arguing some knotty point at a shabby second-hand desk. In another corner, some paymaster or quartermaster perhaps was energetically endeavoring to explain to his colonel or major-general how apparent discrepancies in his accounts could be explained; and elsewhere, soldiers were trying to get a furlough from some officer—women to get a pass to visit son, husband, or brother, who was sick or wounded—or a hundred other questions were being discussed, as freely and with as little reserve as if no listener was within five miles.

"Into the midst of this crowd, every now and then, would dash a courier, booted and spurred, splashed with mud from head to foot, and evidently at the end of a long, anxious ride. A whisper to the lad at the door, and into the sacred presence he is ushered at once. In a few minutes he is out and off again. No unexpected news, no plan discovered any hesitation about what is to be done, evidently."

In February 22nd 1862, a Private Robert Kean (0f the 11th Virginia in Suffolk) was commissioned a Captain in the army and joined the staff of General Randolph as his assistant adjutant-general. In March 1862, General Randolph became Hon. Randolph, the 3rd Secretary of War. Capt. Kean being his young nephew-by-marriage was hired to be the Head of the Bureau of War (one of nine divisions of the War Department). Colonel Kean describes the War Department located in Mechanics Hall, as an old brick building; its great halls and lecture rooms were now converted into offices. He states, that the offices of the President, Cabinet, Treasury and State are housed in the custom-house on Main Street.

Colonel Kean described the functions of the War Department in 1862 as follows: "under the direction and control of the President, had charge of all matters connected with the army and the Indian tribes. Kean was now the head of one of the nine bureaus in the department; two more were staffed after he arrived. Samuel Cooper, ranking general of the Confederacy, served throughout the war as adjutant and inspector general. His office was responsible for the Department's orders and commands, army records, installations and supplies, and the inspection of all army personnel.

An old man and an intimate of the President, Cooper was frequently the target of sharp criticism.

He commented further on the Confederate General Staff: "Colonel Abraham C. Myers was quartermaster-general, and Colonel Lucius B. Northrop was commissary-general of subsistence. Their jobs of furnishing the army with food, clothing, and camp supplies naturally elicited suspicion of graft and profiteering. Their personal conduct and personalities were not conducive to allaying criticism, and they too were constantly under fire. Myers was replaced by General Alexander R. Lawton in August 1863 but Northrop hung on until almost the end of the war. Dr. Samuel P. Moore was surgeon-general. For a time, Major Josiah Gorgas, a talented administrator, headed both engineering and ordnance bureaus, but soon found ordnance a full time job. Thereafter, Captain Alfred Lewis Rives and Colonel Jeremy F. Gilmer alternately served as chief engineer. Isaac M. St. John served admirably as superintendent of the Nitre and mines."

Richmond's defense rested on the too young to join, and the too old to serve, and was reinforced by Government bureau clerks, and local workers from the iron works and shipyard. Most of the blacks (nearly 5,000) were used to build fortifications and another 2,500 were employed to work on the railroads. 5

The stage was set and all the actors awaited their que, the curtain was raising, this play would be a performance of the century . . . . the Show on Broadway continued for 3 more years, until the audience was exhausted. 5, 10, 11, 12, 13

BRIGADIER GENERAL SAMUEL COOPER, C.S.A.

Confederate War Department, and the Preparations for War

In December 1860, the first guns roared signaling the beginning of the War for Southern Independence! The state military forces of South Carolina took charge of the land batteries surrounding Charleston harbor and rained shot and shell down upon the large brick U.S. fort in the center of the harbor. Brigadier General P.T.G. Beauregard had taken command of the shore batteries. South Carolina had announced its succession from the United States of America (i.e. the "Union" was no more!), and demanded the surrender of all federal property to the state. The bombardment continued until Fort Sumter ceased firing and sent up a white flag of truce and surrender. 21, 27, 28

In February 1861, the U.S. congressmen of the eight Deep South states meet in the statehouse at Montgomery, Alabama to form a new provisional government to meet the federal challenge and aggressive actions. A new Congress was formed, slates of provisional executive officers were chosen with Jefferson Davis as President (Ms), and Stephens as Vice President (Ga), and a Chief Supreme Court tabled. Following President Davis' acceptance speech, his office immediately began accepting applications for the many new positions in the new government, both civilian and military. 5, 21

General Samual Cooper, The Adjutant General of the United States Army, War Department, Washington, D.C.; a West Point graduate and military veteran of the Seminole, Creek and the Mexican War. General Cooper had been the adjutant general since 1850, but prior to this he had married a Virginia woman of some wealth and sister of a U.S. Senator, having their home at Cameron Station, Alexandria, Va. The dark war clouds of 1860 made everyone rethink their loyalty to state or nation in the coming conflict. The choice was simple it would be either North or South of the Mason-Dixon Line. It seems this predicament had its greatest impact of the army, as the land force would be the enforcer of Washington edicts to come to quail the revolting southern states. 1, 4, 6

The choice was not "non-slave vs. slave," "East vs. West," the "northern vs. southern tariff," but loyalty and patriotism to ones beloved state! After a long period of consideration (and the fact that he was 60 years of age), finally decided he must throw his lot with his wife's Virginia family. General Cooper informed General Winfield Scott of his resignation from the federal army and vacated the office of Adjutant General in Washington, D.C. 1, 2, 3, 4, 6

Now civilian Samual Cooper decided to give his support to the new southern government organizing in Montgomery, offering them the benefit of his many years of administrative experience and military service. He quietly left Alexandria, Va by train and traveled to Richmond, Raleigh, Charleston, Atlanta to Montgomery. He walked from the station up the hill to the statehouse, and asks to see Mr. Davis (whom he had served with previously, when Davis was the Secretary of War). Upon meeting he offered his services, they were immediately accepted, being appointed by executive order the following day as the new Confederate Adjutant-Inspector General, and confirmed by the Congress thereafter as the senior/ranking Confederate General. The stage was now set!! 5, 6

Shortly, Mr. Walker was appointed and later confirmed as the new Confederate Secretary of War. Both General Cooper and Secretary Walker soon understood that President Jefferson Davis took his new position as Commander-in-Chief very seriously in all matters pertaining to army and navy. It was informally understood that if Virginia succeeded as expected and joined the Confederacy, that the provision capitol would be moved to Richmond. General Cooper did not concern himself with these matters, but realized that manpower was a key issue both for former West Pointers seeking commissions and the volunteers hoping to organize into regiments, and the already existing home guards companies preparing to be recognized by this new government. Cooper began working around the clock to harmonize the chatter and to begin bring order out of chaos (this was his specialty)! 23, 24

So it did not take long for the administrative wheelers to begin turning, then humming as the tempo grew each day, week, month in creating a new military force from the ground up. A number of clerks were hired in the office of the AIG (and War Department) to handle the systematic paper works required in generating forms, forms creating applications, applications giving rise to personnel files, files leading to daily reports . . . . ! Every form had to be designed and printed in bulk; Leger books and Journals had to be designed and printed to tabulate and summarize the data; this was only the tip of the iceberg of the bureaucratic War (where the pen would have the distinct advantage over the sword in winning!). 16, 22, 28

All civilian and former West Pointer officer applications for commission had to be filtered through the Secretary of War for qualification and the President for political sensitivity. Once decided on, the commissioning application was forwarded to the AIG for commission type, rank, branch and unit/position of assignment. Nearly all commissions where granted in the Provisional Army of the CSA, with rank being decided by former army rank (usually one grade advancement in same branch) or the height of recommendation (eg. state governor for Colonels; Congressmen for Majors etc.). 16, 22, 28

From January 1861, many southern states' adjutant general's were already mobilizing state military forces, organizing state regiments and divisions mostly from the home guard, whereas any town of import had its own home guard company, much like the Washington Artillery battery of New Orleans, La. This required each AG to complete an appointment in state service usually for field generals. Field generals traditionally appointed their own staff officers as Captains and Lieutenants (eg. Aides, adjutants, Quartermasters, Chaplains and Medical Directors etc.). Traditionally perused election of regimental officers of Field & Staff for new volunteer units in the ranks of Colonel, Lieutenant-Colonel, and Major—if mustered into state service the AG would record and recognize their commission/appointment. Captains and Lieutenants were elected by their company of about 100 men, and submitted on the Unit Muster for recognition by the AG. Through the four years of warfare, most southern states organized 100 plus Infantry Regiments (totaling around 1,300 in all). 18, 25, 26

General Cooper realized he did not have time to reinvent the wheel of war, so out of expediency he recommended that recruiting agents be sent out to towns throughout the Confederacy to continue to whip up the war fever for ready recruits; temporary generals were appointed to establish Camps of Instruction in each state (in order to turn these raw recruits into basic soldiers of branch). Key generals & staffs had to be located at strategic points in the Confederacy defensive line from the Atlantic Ocean to the Rio Grande River. Small unit fighting was already erupting across the map. 14, 18, 21, 28

In these Camps, recruits were quartered in tents or lentos, feed in company mess, bathing and laundry areas provided, and when available issued uniform parts, sometimes muskets, and a few items of equipment (possibly bayonets, and knifes, etc.). Most recruits came and trained as they were, felt hat, homespun clothes, hunting rifle, bedroll, tin plate & cup—everything needed for marching and battle! Part of the training conducted had to do with drills & ceremonies, cleaning your rifle, unit cooking, and the organizing of battle lines, marching in columns of twos & fours, companies, sections, and finally the regiment. 20, 23, 24

Companies and Regiments had to be taught the flow of paperwork: morning & evening roll calls, necessary unit legers and journals had to be kept, orders, passes & furloughs issued, various letters answered, strength reports forwarded and requisitions filed. As the war progressed the administrative burden grew in complexity, both at the unit level and at the AIG Department. 16, 18, 22, 28

In the beginning, the training was at Company level for about two months with some initial field service. In the infantry branch, by the time ten Companies were trained, the Field & Staff appointed, the regiment would be mustered into state service for active duty (eg. 1st Mississippi Infantry). The state adjutant general would issue orders sending the regiment to a temporary duty station (eg. Camp Plankton). 16, 20, 21, 25, 26

The backbone of the army was the noncommissioned officers—the "Sergeants!" Every item of daily operation had to be conducted by the Sergeant (titles such as First, Second, Third and Fourth; Orderly, Quartermaster, Ordnance, and Commissary). For most of them, it was "on-the-job" training, and as in the beginning they were elected & appointed to their position, (later most promotions were called "Blood Stripes!) 29

As in every army, the regiment needed specialist such as buglers, drummers, musicians, doctors, lawyers, ministers, instructors and managers. So these people in particular were desired and actively sought out for units. 29

Within several months of the war, it was determined by the Confederate government that state regiments would have to be mustered into Confederate Service; and that general officer appointments would have to be controlled by the President, and general officer promotions confirmed by the Confederate Senate, and the Confederate Congress would authorize the number of regiments for Confederate Service. 5, 29

CHAPTER VI

Senior General Samuel Cooper as the Adjutant General in the Confederacy, Richmond, Virginia

Courtesy of the generalcooper.com

Fig. 9. C.S. Adjutant General Samuel Cooper. 1861-1865

GENERAL SAMUEL COOPER, CSA

"In the Service of the Confederacy"

Colonel Samuel Cooper, Adjutant General of the United States Army submitted his army resignation to General Winfield Scott on 7 March 1861, and departed Washington, DC, never to return. 4, 6

He went home to Cameron and packed his bags for a lengthy trip. He boarded a train for Richmond, then to Charleston, on to Atlanta, and finally arriving in Montgomery Station. He had spent a number of days transiting the new Confederacy, seeing the back county of the Carolina's, Georgia and Alabama, its new Capitol. 4, 6

He checked into the Exchange Hotel. It was only a short walk to the statehouse, he felt a festive atmosphere, and could see a band playing and several marching units demonstrating on the main street. He was going to pay a call to the new government of President Davis, and if needed to volunteer his services. He located Davis and they had a short chat about recent developments. Cooper offered his services, and Davis immediately accepted, making him the Adjutant General of the Confederacy, with the rank of Brigadier General, by executive order on 16 May 1861. 5

General Cooper immediately went about organizing his office with the assistance of other military officers. The other officers would become part of his social network and they decided to all go together and rent house the would call "the Ranch," for there stay in Montgomery. The honorable Leroy P. Walker, would be the newly appointed Secretary of War. The Confederate Senate confirmed Cooper's appointment on 31 August 1861. 4

Upon Virginia's succession, the Confederate Capitol would relocate to Richmond. The War Department was given the two story Mechanics Hall (Institute) building on Ninth Street, between Main and Franklin. 5, 10, 12, 13

While working here in Richmond, his son, Samuel Mason would resign his Second Lieutenant's commissioner in Artillery on 5 April 1861, and accept a similar appointment with the Confederate army in August 1861. His daughter, Virginia, would later married a Captain Nicholas Dawson ofVMI. 4, 6

In all actuality, General Samuel Cooper held four roles within the War Department, as Adjutant General, Inspector General, Chief of Staff and Military Advisor to the President. The first two roles were combined by congressional statute as the A&IG; the latter two were maintained as informal relationships with the General Staff, and the Office of the President. 4, 19

Just the first role was mammoth, that of the army Adjutant General (during war time)! Remember even as he had been the U.S. AG, most of his serve there had been during a time of peace, with the exception of the Mexican War. Though he was an exceptional man, he has learned much during those 30 years in staff procedure, therefore making him the most experienced man both of the field and staff, and a most valuable asset to military operations. His success may also belong to the fact that he was a graduate of West Point, and a regular army officer for his entire military career. 2, 3, 4

His whole experience during the war seems to be wrapped in a cloak of government secrecy, even though that was not the case. By his very nature General Cooper was a very quiet person in manner, as well as in speech, and always very humble and a refined gentleman in pubic. There is a not a single report or comment about him that would bring any discredit or blemish. 4, 5

Perhaps his military experience, personal mannerisms and tight family circle made him the perfect soldier. As with most perfect soldiers, he really never had anything of his own, he had married a gentile wife of the aristrocry and inherited a fine home, his handsome son was an officer in the army, and his lovely daughter had married likewise to an officer of VMI. 4

As the Adjutant General, many of his daily activities became standardized throughout the Confederate Army, covering the twelve key operations: records management, military regulations, General & Special Orders, Telegraphic Communications, procuring Officers, recruiting & training manpower, management of troops & units, conducting in-field inspections, reports management and finally handling separations—deceased claims, disabilities, discharges and resignations, to include Forms and Office Management. 15

Other staff actions conducted outside the AG's Department was hospitalizations, pay, substance, feed & fodder, and issuance of uniforms, clothing, equipment, arms and ammunitions. 15

All military units of the army conducted the following related functions through unit adjutants: leaves, furloughs (recruiting & medical), passes and special travel documents; musters, daily orders ledger & reports journal and correspondence (various recommendations and requests); unit parades, marching, Arms Inspections, drill instruction, and discipline (Military Justice). 30, 31, 32

The AG's Department administered the following functions throughout the war:

1. Records Management: Cooper took great care in the maintenance of the official records, files and books of his office, as if his first professional order of business was the preservation of facts. Second, he was ensured that all details where carefully filed and a permanent reference file of all orders was maintained chronologically.
   (See Appendices)
2. Military Regulations: Cooper took pride in his expertness and thoroughness in writing military doctrine, he was responsible for there being a military standard created by his own works on militia's and there formations, and had

been in way use since 1850. He willing gave his advice to the Secretary, the President and the Congress on these matters for law. (See Appendix "B")

3. General & Special Orders: Cooper began utilizing the General Order with the formation of the Confederate Army, these orders were permanent and published under his authority, and given wide distribution throughout the army; while Special Orders were usually of a temporary nature. Both had the impact of regulation, and were effective immediately upon receipt. (See Appendix "B")
4. Telegraphic Communications: Cooper kept the telegraph lines busy around the clock as there impact was immediate; the messages sent from the A & IGO covered just about every operational issue; from unit moves, officer appointments, battle plans, concerns, grips and recommendations. This was probably the first massive use of electronically communications over vast distances. (See Table-1)
5. Officer Procurement: The greatest single source of southern military officers were those regular military officers who where West Point graduates, and who with conscience resigned there commissions (and of course General Cooper was one himself). Requests for appoint-ments in the Confederate Army skyrocketed in 1861. Nearly 300 former officers applied for immediate service. These officers were either commissioned in the permanent Army of the Confederate States (ACSA) or the temporary Provisional Army of the Confederate States (PACS). Officers were also being accepted from Private Military Academies, State Guards and Home guard units. It should be noted State AG's were also procuring officers for state military forces being authorized and organized. The Virginia Military Institute (VMI) was probably the closest things to a West Point in the Confederacy. 5, 21, 33, 39 (See Appendix "D")
6. Recruiting & Training Manpower: Cooper from the beginning knew that recruiting and training would be paramount in a full national mobilization of manpower. Senior temporary officers where appointed to go to specific points and begin receiving civilians for military instruction, lesser temporary officers were be sent out as recruiting agents, especially along the border states. It should be noted that State AG's were also enlisting soldiers and setting up instruction camps for state military forces being authorized and organized. 8, 20, 25, 26
7. Troop & Unit Management: Not only were commissions being granted for specific grades (the President for the nation; Governors for there respective states). In addition to this, appointments had to be generated to all the various levels of command, from Commanders to field & staff, and support units. Generally the practice of electing officers of volunteer units

had been accepted such as regiments and companies. Commanders had the authority to appoint temporary officers to fill unit vacancies, but all officers had to be approved by the A & IGO. All Confederate general officers had to be approved by President Davis and confirmed by the Confederate Senate (1862-1865). 5, 16, 22, 25, 26, 28 (See Appendix "B")

8. Conducting in-field Inspections: Cooper authorized numerous field inspections or investigations by field inspectors of his office, depending on various circumstances. (See Appendices)
9. Reports Management: All units were initially mustered into Confederate Service, and usually an annual Muster was required. Monthly Unit & Command Strength Reports and after-action battle reports flow in on a continual basis. (See Appendix "C")
10. Separations: All separation was handled on a case-by-case basis. Each had to be investigated and endorsed by the chain-of-command, and based on the facts were acted upon. Separations began from the first day, and continued until the end of the war. Separations covered death claims, disability (unfit for duty), discharge (expiration of enlistment) and resignations of officers (for the good of the service), throughout the Confederate army. (See Appendix "D")
11. Forms Management: Cooper was in-charge of directing form development, publishing and use. It is apparent that thousands of forms were utilized to run his office and management the administration of the army. This was probably the first massive use of forms and fill-in letters. (See Appendix "C")
12. Office Management: As in most administrative situations Cooper or his chief clerk was responsible for keeping his office staffed, trained, maintained, and supplied. (See Table of Office of the A&IG)

All of the above mentioned functions of the Adjutant General's Department had only one purpose, "to win the war and preserve the peace!"

To do this, General Cooper had to succeed at number of major missions: to create a manpower resource; to develop an organization hierarchy to support field armies; to acquire aggressive field army leadership; to defend the Confederacy and to destroy Union armies or invade the Union were feasible.

Well, this was Cooper's knowledge base?! His first mission would be to use his small office and staff—first in Montgomery then later Richmond, to create a manpower resource of a million men from across the Confederacy during the first six months. He was helped in this, by the fact that the south had been swamped with "War Fever" since the firing on Fort Sumter in December 1860. Southern patriotism was running wide and recruits were eager to join of all ages. 5, 10, 12, 13

The various Confederate states were ahead of Cooper, in that they had begun to expand there own State Adjutant General Departments to appoint officers, organize units and create local armies in January 1861. President Davis was aware of this and eager to appointed Cooper in May 1861 as the A & IG, he knew it would require a "full national mobilization" and to that end immediately went to work contracting point men as recruiting agents and instruction camp developers for training. The men and camps were not in operation until June 1861. Most instructional camps operated for 6 to 8 weeks to fully training raw recruits into 100 man infantry companies, and organize 10 infantry companies (A thru K) into an infantry or cavalry regiment, or an artillery battery of 2 to 4 guns. Instructors were either veterans of the Mexican War or former regular service. Everyone involved in these operations would soon take a position in the Confederate army.

All units mustered into Confederate service had to be preauthorized in numbers and branch of service. It should be noted that all officers appointed by states had to be re-commissioned by the Confederacy, and all units to be transferred to Confederate service had to be reauthorized as above. 25, 26

It has been stated in the UDC Confederate Hand-Book, that the total effective Confederate field force never grew larger that 500,000 men during the war (this number excludes state troops, home guards and militias). 17

For the first couple of years, state governors were eager to transfer state troops to Confederate service (for the duration of the war), but in the latter years began holding state troops and militia's for state defense. All thirteen Confederate states organized, over 800+ regiments for the Confederate army. It is a fact the State of North Carolina furnished the greatest number men and regiments than any other. 16, 22, 25, 28

After the war fever began to die off, and the reality of combat casualties set in, overall southern recruitment began to wane. Cooper recommended that a defacto conscription service be put in place to keep the manpower pipeline open during more desperate times. 35, 36

At this point Cooper's second mission, was to develop an organization hierarchy to support field armies; in order words to create an effective chain-of-command. Assigning regiments to brigades, brigades to divisions, later divisions to corps, and corps to armies in the field. Cooper attempted to organize 5 to 8 regiments from a state, to a like brigade commander; on the other hand 3-4 local brigades were assigned to divisions on the basis of need. In the beginning, a number of divisions were recognized as field armies. 25, 26

It was reported that 18 such divisions (i.e. armies) were in the field in 1861. They had acquired geographical names, in the East: Army of the Peninsula, Shenandoah, Potomac, Northwest and Kanawha; in the West: Army of Eastern Kentucky, Pensacola, Mobile, East Tennessee-Kentucky, Central Army of Kentucky, West Tennessee-Mississippi, Middle Tennessee, Mississippi and Army of the West; in the Far

West: Army of Louisiana, Missouri State Guard, Missouri, and New Mexico. 27 (See Appendices)

His third mission was to acquire aggressive field army leadership. Apparently there was a huge leadership pool to draw from, mostly West Point graduates and former regular officers. The largest problem became personality conflicts between various followings, such as Generals Beauregard, Bragg, and J.E. Johnston. Too many good Generals were lost in combat such as: A.S. Johnson, Polk, Pickett, Jackson, Stewart and so forth. 33, 34

In terms of command leadership, it was both "trial & error" and "On the Job" training, as there had not been a major war since 1846. Some of these early commanders were not successful, like General Wise, Floyd, Marshall, Harper, Bonham, Garrett, Sibley, Zollicoffer, Twiggs, and A.S. Johnson; other rose and fell according to their misfortunes, General Beauregard, Pemberton, Bragg and Hood. 33, 34

The Confederate congress in late 1861assisted by creating an army rank structure, were as Brigadier General would command brigades, Major General would command division, Lieutenant General would command a corps, and a (full) General would command an Army. The latter to ranks were considered temporary, as long as one commanded a corps or army. 27 (See Appendices)

By 1862, there was a process of consolidation of area forces. In the East they became the Army of Northern Virginia; in the West the Army of Tennessee; and in the Far West, the Army of the Trans-Mississippi. Three of the previously mentioned divisions/armies were disbanded (e.g. Kanawha, Eastern Kentucky, and Western Tennessee-Mississippi) and there troops and units were assigned elsewhere as fillers. 17, 27 (See Appendices)

Cooper's last mission: to defend the Confederacy, destroy Union armies and invade the Union were feasible; was like a roller-coaster ride and the hardest to achieve without supernatural powers! His armies and their leadership were unable to hold West Virginia, Kentucky, Missouri and New Mexico for defense; but as three of these were also failed invasion conquest later, not to forget costs of the invasion of Ohio, Maryland and Pennsylvania. 14, 21

As with the other agencies of the Confederate War Departments, General staff: Quartermaster, Ordnance, Commissary, Paymaster, and Medical, they struggled continuously to support the field armies throughout the war to a point of national exhaustion. There success was great in face of the odds. 30, 31, 32

General Cooper did not allow any of this to deter his goal, to create field armies from nothing and guarantee there success in the field. To this end, he was a friend and confidant to everyone, the soldiers, the generals, the governors, the Secretaries, the President, the Congress, and the citizens of the nation. And even in this, he and his family suffered their personal losses, the day to day problems of survival, and surrounded by a continuously crumbling environment, until the last blow—at nation's end! 4, 5

1861 Montgomery, AL Sec. War L.P. Walker★	1863 Richmond, VA Sec. War J.A. Seddon★	1865 (-) Danville, VA Sec. War J.C. Breckenridge

OFFICE OF THE ADJUTANT & INSPECTOR GENERAL CONFEDERATE STATES ARMY

Field and Staff—Headquarters, Provisional capitol, Montgomery, Alabama
General Samuel Cooper (16 May 61), Adjutant-Inspector General

Assistant Adjutant General—Executive Officer
Orderly Sergeant

Commissions & Promotions Branch
Lieutenant-Colonel Edward A. Palfrey ( )
Assistant Adjutant General

Transferors & Separations Branch
Lieutenant-Colonel John Withers ( )
Assistant Adjutant General

Recruiting & Instruction Branch
(Bureau of Conscription)
Brigadier General John S. Preston ( ) South Carolina
Assistant Adjutant General

Strength Reports Branch
Clerk

Orders & Files Management Branch
Clerk

Military Operations Branch
Clerk

Bureau of Exchange (POW)
Colonel Robert Ould ( ) Virginia
Signal Branch / Corps
Major William Norris ( )

Headquarters, Commandant Branch
Officer in Charge
Supply & Transportation Branch
NOC in charge
Local Details Branch
NCO in charge

CHAPTER VII

General Samuel Cooper as Chief of the General Staff and Military Advisor to the President

Courtesy of the Confederate Publishing Co.

Fig. 10. Confederate Presidential Military Advisors, 1861-65

GENERAL SAMUEL COOPER, CSA

Confederate General Staff. and Military Operations

In General Cooper's role as Military Advisor to the President or as the "Presidential" Chief of Staff, in either case he earned the title, especially during the first three years of the war. He was at his best at the Battle of First Manassas and continued to benefit the operational outcomes up to Battle of Chickamauga. (All top generals had an opportunity to advise). 37, 38, 39

He was the right man for the time! He was educated in Engineering, trained in basic artillery. Cooper had already served as a Military Assistant to three U.S. Presidents, served as a Chief of Staff. His experience was wide and varied, included a great many of Indian campaigns and the Mexican war. He had tour Western Defenses for several years and wrote a technical manual known as "Cooper's Tactics" used widely by the volunteers and militia. He had also worked with then Secretary of War Jefferson Davis for four years. 4, 6, 7, 8

No one in the Confederacy could top those credentials, not even President Davis. Not even other senior officers coming from federal service were only a shadow compared to him in overall experience, such as Colonel A.S. Johnson and Brigadier General J.E. Johnston. 33, 34

As can be seen below General Lee was the Star field general, but this was as much do to great tactics and strategy on his part, as it was paramount for the General Staff under General Cooper, to deliver the war material such as, ammunition, food, fodder, tools, replacement troops and unit reinforce-ments, medical supplies, and sometimes long range intelligence on enemy troop shifts, at the right place—at the right time. This was certainly more easily done in the eastern theater of operations than in the west. 35, 36

Every army in the field requires out of necessity a supply train, which would have a designated source of supply (usually a rail head or center). This supply line was maintained by hundreds of wagons, horse or mule teams and teamsters to keep them moving around the clock, regardless of weather or battle conditions. The cavalry out of necessity had to sometimes escort or otherwise protect these supply trains while stationary and on route. 35, 36

An example of the problem was highlighted by General Sibbly's ill faded New Mexico invasion, especially in a desolate area of desert; the invasion was otherwise successful, but failed at its peak due to the loss of its supply trains that were otherwise unprotected and destroyed. All generals understand that "an army lives by its stomach." 14, 21

Twelve victorious battles of the Confederacy, shared by Cooper & Generals:

- ★ First Manassas,VA—21 July 1861
  General's Beauregard & J. Johnston

- ★ Wilson Creek, MO—10 August 1861
  General Price

- ★ First Winchester,VA—25 May 1862
  General Jackson

- ★ Gaines' Mill,VA—27 June 1862
  General Lee

- ★ Second Manassas,VA—28-30 August 1862
  General Lee

- ★ Fredericksburg,VA—11-15 December 1862
  General Lee

- ★ Chancellorsville,VA—30 April / 6 May 1863
  General Lee

- ★ Chickamauga, GA—18-20 September 1863
  General Bragg

- ★ Mansfield, LA—8 April 1864
  General Taylor

- ★ Cold Harbor,VA—31 May / 12 June 1864
  General Lee

- ★ Petersburg,VA—15-18 June 1864; and the Crater,VA—30 July 1864
  General Lee

CHAPTER VIII

The AG Records Branch and the Regimental Paper Trail of the Inspector General

GENERAL SAMUEL COOPER, CSA

Adjutant-General's Records Branch and the Regimental Paper Trail of the Inspector General

The life blood of General Cooper's bureaucracy in Richmond was sourced by the 800 plus army regiments (adjutants) and over 8,000 Orderly Sergeants in the Confederate army stretched over 1,500 miles of territory.

As an example of this "paper trail," we'll consider three such combat infantry regiments: 2nd Kentucky, 27th Mississippi and the 46th North Carolina. Each unit organized at different stages of the mobilization process. 30, 31, 32

All three infantry regiments were authorized and commissioned under different circumstances.

The 27th Miss. Volunteers was authorized as an augmentation to the Army of Pensacola commanded by General Bragg and headquartered in Mobile. The 10 rifle companies were requested from the adjutant general of Mississippi as filer for a new regiment. The officership, namely a Colonel Jones as commander, had already been determined by the President for commissioning the 27th Miss. in Mobile. This unit had been armed with the older smooth boar rifle muskets. 31

Whereas, the 2nd Ky. was authorized by congress, and General Cooper, A&IG sent volunteer recruiters to towns in Kentucky, and a General Withers was appointed to receive recruits from Kentucky and establish a Camp of Instruction in Tennessee. As the recruits arrived they were organized into to 10 rifle companies, the President would make sure they were commanded by a select set of Kentuckians, namely one Colonel Roger Hanson (a CSA recruiter, and a member of the Kentucky State Guard). Two Kentucky regiments (2nd & 3rd) would be organized into a Kentucky Brigade (with other regiments as they became available), also to be commanded by a presidential selection of General John C. Breckinridge (a former U.S. Vice President) and commissioned in Bowling Green, Kentucky in November 1861. This unit lacking state support, was also inadequately armed with a wide variety of weapons, and had to be rearmed from the battlefield. 32

Then, the 46th N.C. was authorized by the state adjutant general. Recruits and rifle companies were sent to Camp Mangum near Raleigh, for instruction and organization as North Carolina State Troops (NCST). The regimental leadership was commissioned as state officers. When completed and ready for commissioning the regiment, it was offered by Governor Vance to President Davis. The President accepted and the regiment was sworn into Confederate service for the duration of the war. The regiment was transferred to Camp Lee, Richmond for further assignment to the Army of Northern Virginia. This unit was well armed with the latest Federal muskets. 30

The 27th Mississippi Infantry Regiment Volunteers was probably a good example of this "paper trial" while operating in the field under all hazards, weather, battle conditions, in camp and constant movement. An Orderly Sergeant by the name of Robert Amos Jarman, Company K, from Aberdeen, Mississippi kept fairly concise diary of these activities. 31

In his diary he speaks of five required company musters that had to be letter perfect; there was the initial organization muster (Aberdeen) 1861, later he would complete another muster at Augusta, Georgia 1863; again following the battle of Jonesboro 1864; then 1865 while marching across Tennessee at Rienzi, and again marching east at Montgomery, finally upon arrival at Smithfield, N.C. (these musters were consolidated up the chain of command until the reached the A&IG in Richmond, Virginia). 31

He speaks of numerous daily report calls; receiving General Orders from the A&IG, Richmond; issuing passes while in camp in Tennessee in 1863, and in Georgia in 1864. Men were usually given furloughs as either a reward (i.e. Recruiting) or rehabilitation (i.e. Sick or hospital leave), he made four entries: one in the summer 1863, and one in winter 1863, and one for illness in winter 1864. He notes that company punishment was given several times for "Dirty Guns," and for "Unlawful Forging!" Most promotions—were blood promotions and announced at First Call each morning. He as well carried out the daily orders of the regiment, and forwarded requisitions for all manner of material that may be available. Sgt. Jarman had several jobs to perform as the regiment, and company grew smaller from casualties, served also as First Sergeant and Drillmaster, too. 31 (See Appendix "B-C-D")

So it can be seen that everything that ended up in the A&IG, Richmond began in a company or regiment somewhere in the army, from some frontier.

CHAPTER IX

Bankruptcy and Empty Cupboards, Crippling the Army with an Uncertain Future

Fig. 11. General-in-Chief Robert E. Lee, 1865

General R. E. Lee at the end of the war. *U.S. Army photograp from the painting by Sidney E. Dickinson*

ADJUTANT AND INSPECTOR GENERAL'S OFFICE,
Richmond, February 6, 1865.

GENERAL ORDERS,
No. 3.

I. The following Act of Congress is published for the information of the army:

An Act to provide for the appointment of a General in Chief of the Armies of the Confederate States.

"SECTION 1. The Congress of the Confederate States of America do enact, That there shall be appointed by the President, by and with the advice and consent of the Senate, an officer, who shall be known and designated as 'General in Chief,' who shall be ranking officer of the army, and as such, shall have command of the military forces of the Confederate States.

SEC. 2. That the act providing a staff for the General who may be assigned to duty at the Seat of Government, is hereby repealed, and that the General in Chief, who may be appointed under the provisions of this act, shall have a staff not less than that now allowed a General in the field, to be assigned by the President, or to be appointed by him, by and with the advice and consent of the Senate." [Approved 23d January 1865.]

II. General ROBERT E. LEE having been duly appointed General in Chief of the Armies of the Confederate States, will assume the duties thereof, and will be obeyed and respected accordingly.

III. General Orders, No. 23, of 1864, is hereby revoked.

By order.

S. COOPER,
Adjutant and Inspector General.

Courtesy of the National Archives

Fig. 13. A&IG General Order #2, dated February 6, 1865

GENERAL SAMUEL COOPER, C.S.A.

General-in-Chief Robert E. Lee
Commander of all Confederate Forces

"A future of uncertainty"

General Cooper's prospects were indeed looking very dim by January 1865. He had done his job well, perhaps too well! The southern countryside had been stripped for the sake of "Total War"! Not only stripped, but devastacated and left desolate . . . and deserted. That is real war. Those southern patriots of 1861 had been starved, tortured, bled, disabled and killed by tens of thousands; homes shattered, families dislocated, and a terrible curse descending upon them without reprieve or appeal. 14, 21

This was Cooper's world, his nation, his state, his career and his family! The winter of 1864-1865 was also uniquely break, as well—frozen ground, bear trees, gray cold skies over Richmond; . . . high inflation, scarcity of essentials and the continual ringing of the tocsin bell nearby for communal prayer and forgiveness . . . . The churches were full and the cupboards were empty. 21

The Union army was now but a few miles away, shelling the city at will, moving ever closer; the defenders were fewer—looking lean but determined to hold on for a miracle . . . the Confederate military situation was becoming desperate, seeming to be in retreat on every front . . . . in want of everything, and only having Spring to look forward too! 14, 21, 25

Yes, General Cooper had done his best, yet he reported to his office everyday in the Confederate War Department, to continue his daily routine without showing any emotion or condemnation of its results. He was conjugal with all, and continued his rounds of consultation with the Generals, the Secretary, the President, and the Congress. He knew he had no tricks or miracles only prayer for what was coming . . . soon! 4, 6

Throughout January, February and March 1865, the lights at the executive mansion (White House) and the War Department would burn continuously, with all manner of people visiting Secretary Breckinridge or President Davis for some kind of reassurance or consolation. 5, 40

Throughout this time it would seem that Cooper and his family had considered their options in the face of disaster and national collapse. I believe that General Cooper was quietly organizing and packing his books and files for the eventual evacuation of the city, if General Lee's Army of Northern Virginia could know hold the barricades indefinitely. 6, 16. 28, 40

In the end, General Cooper felt he had several duties remaining: first to evacuate the War Department by train and relocate his office to Danville, Virginia.; second, if things continued to digress, to load his records and files onto wagons and secretly transport them to a farm in Lynchburg, Virginia for storage and protection; and finally to accompany Secretary Breckinridge and President Davis to the end of the line—his last full measure of duty achieved. 6, 16, 28

One might say the Confederacy prayers were answered on Palm Sunday morning that April 1865—to bring the mass suffering to a conclusion. General Lee's couriers arrived at the War Department and at President Davis' church to quietly inform him that the Union army had broken through and that the city could not be defended much longer, and an immediate evacuation was necessary. 18, 21, 40

President Davis, Secretary Breckinridge and General Cooper immediately began the process; the President notified Congress and called a final cabinet meeting, the War Department staff was assembled, and the railroads began making preparations for the government's withdrawal. All government employees were told to stay at there posts, and General Winder the Provost Marshal General took charge of securing the city. 5, 18, 21

At 9:00 p.m. Sunday night, the long trains began to roll out of the Richmond Station west, destination Danville, Virginia. The President and his cabinet, General Cooper and other key government officials were departing hurriedly. Secretary Breckinridge stayed behind for the last train to pickup all the loose ends for the military. The government trains arrived the next morning and went about reestablishing itself in the county courthouse. General Lee's army was already on the move west in three columns. 4, 6, 35

Waiting several days to get word on General Lee's army, the President at a cabinet meeting to move the Confederate government further south between the Confederate Army of Northern Virginia and the Confederate Army of Tennessee. Trains were reloaded, destination Greensboro, North Carolina. 4, 6, 31. 35

Word finally arrived on the following Easter Sunday, April 7th, 1865 that General Lee's army had been outflanked and cutoff near Appomattox's Courthouse, Virginia and had surrendered to General Grant of the Union army. That General Johnston's army was still in full retreat nearing Raleigh, North Carolina. Secretary Breckinridge would go to Durham Station and assist General Johnston's surrender to General Sherman of the Union army. 18, 35

At the Easter Sunday cabinet meeting, it was decided that the movement south would continue immediately by train to Abbeville, South Carolina. By this time, General Cooper's health was in decline, so he asks for a leave of absence from President Davis, and it was granted. Cooper left the party the next day on horseback traveling north, with one last mission ahead of him. 5

The Presidential party continued this time by horses and wagons to Washington, Georgia, having the 2nd Kentucky regiment as escort. In Washington, Georgia, President Davis had his final Council of War and Cabinet meeting giving the cabinet secretaries and other officials a leave of absence, and decided he, his family, aids and a small escort would continue west by horse and wagon. 4, 6, 16, 28

Shortly, the Presidential party was overtaken by Union cavalry and captured at Irving, Georgia. The war had ended, the Confederate government gone, now the armies to the west would seek out there own closure. 14, 21, 32

General Samuel Cooper's final mission upon conclusion of the war was to preserve and protect all Official Confederate army documents in his charge, and to seek a federal official that he might surrender the records in tact for future history. He accomplished this feat in Lynchburg; he was not arrested but given a parole, and retook the oath required of all ex-Confederates. 6, 16. 28

He gather up his family and returned to Cameron Station, Alexandria, Virginia; were he lived out his last years in a servant house, in abstract poverty and illness, till his death (11 years later) on December 3rd, 1876. 46

Courtesy of the Virginia Historical Society

Fig. 12. The General Staff of Lee's Headquarters

TABLE—1

ORDER OF BATTLE CONFEDERATE FORCES
LAST MONTH OF WAR—REORGANIZATION
March 1865

CONFEDERATE FORCES: General in Chief Robert E. Lee
ARMY OF THE CONFEDERATE STATES—C.S.A.

50,000 Men (All Theaters inclusive)

ARMY OF NORTHERNVIRGINIA:
Commanding: General Robert E. Lee (Va)

I CORPS:
Commanding: Lieutenant General Ewell
II CORPS:
Commanding: Lieutenant General Longstreet
III CORPS:
Commanding: Lieutenant General D. H. Hill
IV CORPS:
Commanding: Lieutenant General Anderson
CAVALRY CORPS:
Commanding: Lieutenant General Wade Hampton

ARMY OF TENNESSEE:
Commanding: General Joseph E. Johnston

I CORPS:
Commanding: Lieutenant General William D. Hardee
II CORPS:
Commanding: General P.T.G. Beauregard
III CORPS:
Commanding: General Braxton Bragg
IV CORPS:
Commanding: Lieutenant General Stephen D. Lee
CAVALRY CORPS:
Commanding: Lieutenant General Joseph Wheeler

ARMY OF THE TRANS-MISSISSIPPI (Departments thereof):
Commanding: General Edmund Kirby-Smith

ARMY OF MISSISSIPPI (Departments thereof):
Commanding: Lieutenant General Robert Taylor

W.L.S
RUINS OF CONFEDERATE WAR DEPARTMENT 1865
THE BELLHOUSE FROM WHICH FIRE ALARMS AND TOCSINS WERE RUNG.
THE STANDING MASS WAS CORNER OF ADJUTANT GENERAL COOPER'S OFFICE.

Courtesy of the Last Review

Fig. 18. Ruins of the Confederate War Department building, 1865

PART THREE

"The Twilights Last Gleaming . . . . !"

PROFESSIONALISM & PATRIOTISM WITHOUT REGRETS

CHAPTER X

The Unsung Heroics and Deeds of the Clerks in Gray!

Courtesy of the Virginia Historical Society

Portrait of Taylor, posed in his uniform as lieutenant colonel, C.S. Army. Painted by Thomas C. Cole. (Original in the Virginia Historical Society, Richmond, Va. Reproduced with permission.)

Fig. 15. A Model Assistant AG – COL Walter Taylor, 1865

ASSISTANT ADJUTANT GENERAL'S

"The Unsung Heroics and Deeds of the Clerks in Gray!"

It is estimated that there were over one thousand two hundred assistant adjutant generals appointed in the Confederate States Army, at any one time over the four year period of the war.

Technically speaking, the following military administrators of staff could be placed on this list of hero's and deeds surpassing most officers of the war on either side:

(Full) General Samuel Cooper

(Full) General Robert Edward Lee

(Full) General P.T.G. Beauregard

(Full) General Braxton Bragg

All these general officers had served as aides, administrators, and chiefs of staff, and finally as Presidential Military Advisors (the ultimate position). 34

Most AAG's (adjutants) entered the service as volunteer aid-de-camps or were recruited from the civilian work force or college, and still others were appointed upon the mustering of their unit or regiment. Most adjutant's were commissioned according to there level of organization (e.g. regiments appointed Lieutenants, while brigades-Captains, divisions-Majors, and units above division-Lieutenant Colonel). All recommendations were sent through the chain of command and War Department, to the Adjutant General Cooper. The term "adjutant general" was dropped in lower commands (i.e. Armies and CSA Departments) to prevent confusion, but retained by state military departments. (See Appendix "A")

Most AAG's resisted higher promotion to remain with there commanders, though some were very distinguished and joined a long list of general officers at all levels of command. Some became Chief-of-Staff, and/or temporary wing commanders; others, joined the high profile ranks of Brigade, Division and Corps/Department Commanders. 36, 41, 42

Lieutenant-General Stephen D. Lee

One of the highest ranking general's supporting the Confederate cause was Lieutenant-General Stephen D. Lee (a nephew of General Robert E. Lee), who began his Confederate military career as a Captain, Assistant Adjutant General on the headquarter staff of General P. T. G. Beauregard in Charleston, South Carolina. He was sharp organizer, knowledgeable of military administration, staff procedures, and as a line artillerist. 41

Later, because of his desire for field duty—he received a second commission in-grade, in the branch of Artillery. His Confederate career took him into the Cavalry, and line command up to department commander, and final as a Corps commander of the Army of Tennessee. All too often he was cited for personal bravery and gallantry! 41

Brigadier-General (T) Gilbert Moxley Sorrel

Brigadier-General John Marshall Jones

Brigadier-General W. W. Mackall

All of these general officers were promoted because of unyielding personal bravery, gallantry on the field of combat, efficiency of command, and infatigable zeal for duty! 42

Colonel Robert G. H. Kean
Chief, Bureau of War, War Department

Colonel Walter Taylor
Military Secretary, Lee's Headquarters ANV

Colonel Archer Anderson
Assistant Adjutant General, Holmes Division

These Colonels were promoted above the grade authorized for there duty position because of there unusual abilities as military administrators and as combat officers. Both Gilbert Sorrel and Robert Kean initially tried to get officer appointments from Richmond, and were denied because of the lack of prior military experience (both men served briefly as enlisted soldiers).

Later, each had the good fortune of being at the right place—at the right time; Sorrel joining as a clerk in General Longstreet's staff as a volunteer, and Kean likewise joining as a aide on General Randolph's staff on the Virginia Peninsula. Many serving adjutants were killed in the line of duty. 11, 36

JOHN BELL HOOD
To Paraphrase a Classic Eulogy, "None Led with More Glory than Hood, yet Many Led and There Was Much Glory."

EDMUND KIRBY SMITH
Skilful and Persistent Fighter Against Odds and Ever Indomitable in the Face of Reverses in the Field.

BRAXTON BRAGG
Leader in Three of the Fiercest Battles of the War and Carried the Southern Battle Line to Its Farthest North in the West; A Record of Four Years in the Field.

SAMUEL COOPER
Ranking Officer of the Army. All Commanding Generals Reported to Cooper and Received All Orders from Him. His Post and Duties were those of a Modern Cnief of Staff.

CONFEDERATE GENERALS—FULL RANK
HOOD, KIRBY SMITH, BRAGG AND COOPER

Fig. 16. Confederate High Command

CHAPTER XI

Farewell to Arms General "You were Indeed a Hero!" The staff and men in the ranks morn your passing

Courtesy of the National Archives

Fig. 17. Photo – Final Pose of General Samuel Cooper, 1870

GENERAL SAMUEL COOPER, CSA
1798-1876
"Cooper's Farewell to Arms"

A fate we must all shall . . . .

"His last official act as the Adjutant and Inspector General of the Confederacy was turning over the Official Records of the Confederacy (Confederate States Army) to the United States Government. These records became invaluable contribution to the "War of the Rebellion Official Records of the Union and Confederate Armies." This contribution is said to be Samuel's most lasting contribution to the Confederacy, in overseeing the removal of War Department records from Richmond in April 1865, and protecting them until they could be turned over to Federal authorities in North Carolina (should be Virginia) after Johnston's surrender." 6, 16, 28

According to Samuel Cooper Dawson, his great-grandson, "General Cooper was paroled at Charlotte, North Carolina on May 3, 1865. He moved back into Mecklenburg County, Virginia, where he remained for nearly a year, before returning to his home on Seminary Hill". 4, 9

Upon the family's return, there stood a gray federal Fort William (where the mansion once stood before the war). (Actually the fort had been named Fort Traitor, in dishonor of then Colonel Cooper), but through the efforts of their son-in-law General Frank Wheaton, USA, (the husband of the late Maria Cooper) in 1863 he got the fort's name changed). The Federals had also confiscated the land. The Cooper family took up temporary residence at the nearby Theological Seminary, a former place of worship. After the war, also through the efforts of General Wheaton, a Mr. W.M. Corcoran who had once been befriended by the Cooper's and Mason's when he first arrived in Washington in 1830, felt an unpaid debt towards the family. He not only purchased the property, but fixed up the old Overseer's house in the rear, and gave it back to Mrs. Cooper, as her residence. 4, 9

General Cooper never regained his citizenship, but lived on at Cameron until his death. During the last years of his life, he commenced to write his recollections and incidents and characters during 50 years of military service. He unfortunately, got only to 1852, when he became the Adjutant General of the United States. The book, or biography, ends suddenly at that date, and evidently that was 1876. During this period of time he was also, corresponding with the Southern Historical Society, and with various people concerning his duties at Richmond during the war. Bearing on this, an article from the New Orleans Times-Picayune of September 28, 1869, in which Confederate Losses during the war were detailed in correspondence between

Dr. Joseph Jones, Secretary of the Southern Historical Society and General Cooper were presented. 1, 4, 9

General Fitzhugh Lee made the following observations about Cooper:

"During the four long years in the life of the Confederacy, General Cooper fully discharged the onerous duties confided to him with fidelity, and exactness, a loyalty and an honesty, which, whilst perfectly consistent with his conscientiousness and ability, gave great satisfaction to the army and the country. It is indeed difficult to place a proper estimate upon the value of his service during that trying period, so great was his capacity for work.

Punctiliously and unceasingly he daily discharged the great duties of his office; and at night, when others sought relaxation and rest, in a room in his private residence, his work was steadily carried forward." 7

In a letter from Jefferson Davis (perhaps to General Fitzhugh Lee) . . . the following was given on behalf of General Cooper:

"I am gratified to know that you have under-taken to make a record of the services and virtues of a man than whom none has higher claims upon the regard of all who love the Confederacy. No one presents an example more worth of the emulation of the youth of his country." 5 (See Appendix "D")

"Unmolested at the end of the war, Samuel returned to find his home, Cameron, near Alexandria had been replaced by a Federal fort. Nevertheless, he moved into what had been his overseer's house, and there took up small farming, the remaining of the old hero were quietly and peacefully passed. 9

"As an aged man living a life as a farmer, General Cooper became a soldier in distress. On August 4, 1870, Robert E. Lee, on behalf of General Lawson, Colonel Cole and others, sent Samuel a sum of money. They were able to raise $300 dollars for Samuel. General Lee in a letter to Samuel wrote 'To this sum I have only been able to add $100, but I hope it may enable you to supply some immediate want and prevent you from taxing your strength too much. You must also pardon me for my moving in this matter, and for the foregoing explanation, which I feel obliged to make that you might understand the subject.'" 4, 9

"General Samuel Cooper died upon the 3rd (14th?) of December 1876, in the seventy-eighth year of his age." For many years before his death he was a conscientious and consistent communicant of the Episcopal church," 2, 3, 4, 6, 9

At the burial at Christ Church Cemetery in Alexandria, it was said, "Well done, thou good and faithful servant, enter thou into the joy of the Lord." His bereaved family can indeed find consolation, in their irreparable loss, in the belief: "Blessed are the pure in heart, for they shall see God." 4, 9

CHAPTER XII

The Cooper Legacy for future Armies in Methodologies and Technologies . . .

GENERAL SAMUEL COOPER, C.S.A.

"The Cooper Legacy for Future Armies in Methodologies and Technologies"

I think the Cooper legacy to military develop, as gone for to long as an unsung father of modern military administration and staff procedures.

Colonel Cooper, U.S.A. maintained a peacetime Federal army of some 10,000 soldiers and less than 50 installations and outposts. He mobilized that army for small Indian campaigns and the Mexican-America War with great success. He practically trained ALL the officers and many soldiers for the great Civil War, and there ability surpassed all expectations. 4, 14, 21

General Cooper, C.S.A. mobilized a war time Confederate army of over 1 million soldiers and more that 250 installations and 1,000 outposts across a 2,000 mile frontier. He is responsible for creating some 21 field armies and 5 theater armies, and his methods were principally communication, legislation, regulation, consultation, and adherence to the Chain of command, in other words "military staff procedures." He was a soldier of great administrative experience and resource. He had strength of character and commitment to deal with 500 subordinate generals. 34, 35

It is said that he set the standard for all future Adjutant Generals, in terms of efficiency and effectiveness. He grasps the big picture of the problems as related to organizing, leading, arming, supporting and maintaining large armies in the field. His office was the first modern approach to warfare in the twentieth century. By the fact that he held three major roles, as Adjutant General (a detail man), Chief of the General Staff (a man of considerable persuasion) and Presidential Military Advisor (and a known quantity) reflects that he was a man of strength and means of authority. 5

He was well known for having a mind for detail and strong memory personal impressions. As far as a manpower goes: he personally know nearly every West Point graduate (1845-1860), he knew he must recruit all resources (locally, state and foreign), and he knew he had to have a pipeline from which to draw continuously from, volunteers, hospital rolls, conscription and Negro impressments, and stop-loss measures were undertaken.

He was keen on military organization, and providing the best leadership available; but everything had to be by the book, structured basic training, training manuals, proper garrisons and camps maintained, manning tables (via the unit muster rolls), respecting unit integrity and the judgments of his officers. He authorized promotions based on vacancy or field promotions temporarily during battle. Every action was accountable, controlled and authorized by orders; be it enlistments, transfers, leaves, movements, medical or courts marital, even care for the deceased. Units were banned together and made seamless, with the strict use of the chain of command.

Unit movements were made rapidly using messengers, courier or telegraph and by employment wagons, railways or boats. Battle reports and Casualty reports were sent immediately and used to update battle estimates and muster roll records. Tactical and Strategic maps were updated continuously.

The General Staff made every effort to comfort, medicate, feed, pay, arm, equip, uniform and provide transportation to the men I the field, and it was done with great success, until the national base becomes exhausted.

The Vietnam Era Adjutant General had many of the same problems as Cooper. Some of these problems were self made, such as the 1 years deployment limitation (this was similar to the Volunteer Enlistment for 1 year); the lack of local support (this was similar to the need to invade enemy strongholds and continue the advance); special problems with environment and diseases (this was similar to coping with weather, dysentery and wounds). The annual R&R (most Confederate soldiers were given either long-term furloughs or short passes). Most Confederates killed would have been considered "MIA's" today, but "casualty estimates" were quiet good.

Cooper utilized every available method to being about a general mobilization from scratch. From an administrative standpoint, he used the best ink, stationary and printing presses (for bulk distribution); clerks skilled in calligraphy (for penmanship and reproduction), all registers of correspondence, orders, reports, returns and other communications in bound Ledgers & Journals (for tracking); standardized Numbered Ordering system, Coded Bundles Filing system, a published set of regulation and doctrine, and most responses by endorsement on correspondence. For money he was forced to use the "full faith and Credit of the Nation!"

I feel his systematic approach to record keeping, assured that he could find any individual soldier within the Confederate army. The evidence is found not only in historical records, but in the National Archives—Confederate Records. By a simple compilation of these documents one could establish a soldier's individual's military personnel file (similar to the army's 201 File). (Even in this day and time, with the help of computers—orders are mislaid, and individual soldiers are hard to find?) 16, 28

As for technology, the nineteenth century was booming! Arms & Ordnance, Medicine, Transportation, Communications, and Naval. The technology of administration was changing as well, better quality paper stock, faster drying inks, sharper engraving, faster printing presses, gas lighting, the use of preprinted forms, the adding machine, electronic communications, and of course the factory system, and the all out use of rail systems. (See Appendices)

So in General Cooper's department we can find all the modern facets of the Adjutant General, Office of Personnel Operations/G-1: 15 (See Appendix "A")

Officer Procurement, Officer Evaluations Reports, Officer Transfers & Reassignments, Officer Vacancy & Promotion Management (MTO&E); Officer Promotion Boards; Congressional Inquiries. 15 (See Appendix "B & D")

Personnel Actions Management for Separation (Resignation, Courts marital proceedings, Disability, Unfitness, Hardship). 15 (See Appendix "D")

Personnel Records Management: (Enlistment / Commission, Promotions (Temporary / Permanent), Assignments, Special Duties, Hospital Roll, Muster Status, Disposition). 15 (See Appendix "B, C & D")

Administrative Services Management: Regulations, Orders, Training & Doctrine, Circulars and Memorandums; Reproduction, Distribution, Filing Mail, Electronic communications, Messengers & Couriers Service, Classified Documents, and freight. 15 (See Appendix "B")

Casualty Reporting: Nearly all casualties were accounted for, either thru commander notification, Muster Roll returns, or Daily Hospital Reports. 15 (See Appendix "C")

★Awards and Decorations: This was handled at the lowest level of command, usually at the Regiment. Recognition varied from a promotion, or appointment, of report of Gallantry & Bravery, or being a Flag Bear, or simply given a furlough home. 15 (See Appendix "B & D")

★Reception Stations & Replacement Detachments: Processing civilians, enlistment, initial records (Muster), personal identification (passes), initial pay voucher, medical check-up, issue of arms, equipment and clothing available, and basic training and camp support (i.e. tent & rations), and a mode of transport (i.e. orders & marching) forward. ★(Regimental Adjutants).

So it seems from General Cooper's experience both in peace and war, we have been able to use the so called "Trial & Error" and / or "Lessons Learned" from this his methods (paper) and his technology (stubby pencil) of that era, we now have come to call the last line of resistance or backup! 15

Through his activities as documented, he was instrumental to set the stage for larger more complex armies. I believe his results brought about the design and implementation of such activities within the army: Office of Personnel Operations (OPO), the Manpower G-1, the Personnel Service Division (PSD), the Administration Company, the Personnel Services Company (PSC), Battalion S-1/adjutant, the Personnel Command & Centers, in both doctrine and table of organization & equipment. 15

So even though 150 years have passed, and we are caught up in runaway technologies, the old methods still prevail when all else fails. General Cooper gave it, 50 years of his life without any consideration of pension! Paramount was to do his duty to God, State (Country) and Family—labeled him a Professional and Patriot. (There motto in Latin was "Deo Vindice!")

The modern motto of the Adjutant General Corps / Regiment is: "1776—Defend and Serve" (in 1861 it was the same Defend and Serve) . . . . !

All personnel operations in the United States Army are now covered by Field Manual One. 15, 29

End.

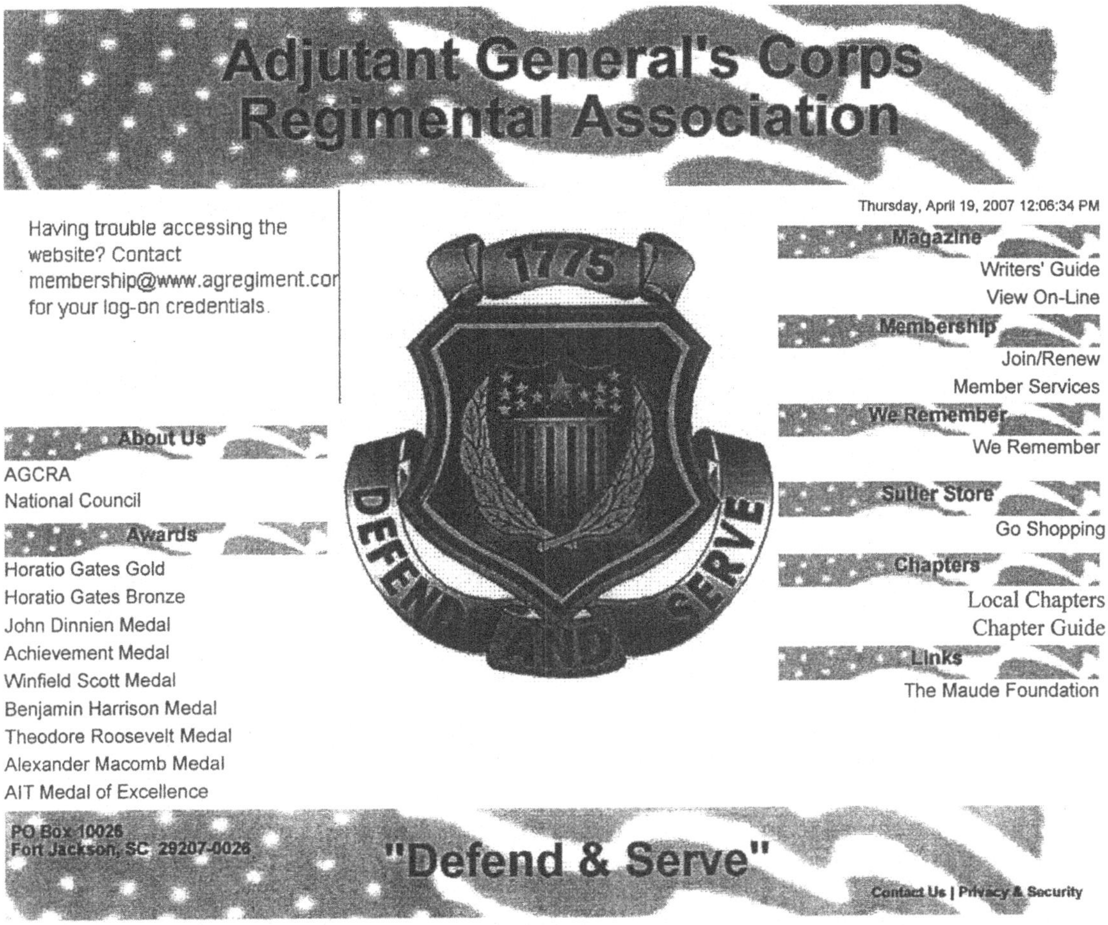

Adjutant General's Corps Regimental Association

Thursday, April 19, 2007 12:06:34 PM

Having trouble accessing the website? Contact membership@www.agregiment.co[m] for your log-on credentials.

1775

DEFEND AND SERVE

About Us

AGCRA

National Council

Awards

Horatio Gates Gold

Horatio Gates Bronze

John Dinnien Medal

Achievement Medal

Winfield Scott Medal

Benjamin Harrison Medal

Theodore Roosevelt Medal

Alexander Macomb Medal

AIT Medal of Excellence

Magazine

Writers' Guide

View On-Line

Membership

Join/Renew

Member Services

We Remember

We Remember

Sutler Store

Go Shopping

Chapters

Local Chapters

Chapter Guide

Links

The Maude Foundation

PO Box 10026
Fort Jackson, SC 29207-0026

"Defend & Serve"

Contact Us | Privacy & Security

Courtesy of the US Army, Adjutant General Corps Regiment Assn.

Fig. 19. General Samuel Cooper's Modern Day Legacy (US Army)

APPENDICES

Manuscripts Department
Library of the University of North Carolina
at Chapel Hill
SOUTHERN HISTORICAL COLLECTION

#2482
SAMUEL COOPER PAPERS
Summary

NOTE: A more complete finding aid for this collection is available at the Southern Historical Collection. Contact staff at: (919)962-1345 (telephone); (919)962-4452 (FAX); mss@email.unc.edu.

Cooper, Samuel, 1798-1876.
Papers, 1775-1893.
96 items.

Native of New Jersey, adjutant general in the U.S. Army, and adjutant general and inspector general in the Confederate Army.

Reminiscences, scattered correspondence, and other papers of Cooper and papers of his father, Major Samuel Cooper (1759-1809) of Massachusetts. Cooper's reminiscences cover the period 1818-1852 and discuss army operations in the Second Seminole War, 1841-1842, on the Texas frontier, 1851, and against Indians in Texas. Correspondence of Cooper chiefly concerns the U.S. War Department before the Civil War and home life in Fairfax County, Va. It includes eight letters, 1853-1854, from Capt. Lucius Bellinger Northrop (1811-1894) to Cooper concerning Northrop's sick furlough from the U.S. Army; and two letters, 1863 and 1864, concerning the military situation around Wilmington, N.C., and Richmond, Va., respectively. Papers of Major Samuel Cooper (1759-1809) include brief reminiscences of his Revolutionary War service, including the Battle of Lexington and the Boston Tea Party.

ONLINE CATALOG TERMS:
- Autobiographies--Massachusetts.
- Autobiographies--Virginia.
- Boston Tea Party, 1773.
- Confederate States of America. Army--Officers--Correspondence.
- Cooper, Samuel, 1759-1809.
- Cooper, Samuel, 1798-1876.
- Fairfax County (Va.)--Social life and customs--19th century.
- Indians of North America--Texas--History--19th century.
- Indians of North America--Wars--1815-1875.
- Lexington, Battle of, 1775.
- Massachusetts--Biography.
- Northrop, Lucius Bellinger, 1811-1894.
- Richmond (Va.)--History--Civil War, 1861-1865.
- Seminole War, 2nd, 1835-1842--Personal narratives.
- Texas--History--1846-1950.
- United States--History--Revolution, 1775-1783--Personal narratives.
- United States. Army--Officers--Biography.
- United States. War Dept.--History--19th century.
- Virginia--Biography.
- Wilmington (N.C.)--History--Civil War, 1861-1865.

THE BLOODY SIXTH: a Regiment Is Organized

Personnel

"Before it went to the field each North Carolina regiment needed a colonel, lieutenant colonel, a major, an adjutant, one surgeon and two assistant surgeons, one assistant quartermaster, an assistant commissary sergeant, and ten companies of troops. Each company had a captain, one first lieutenant, two second lieutenants and on the average, from fifty to eighty men. Each regiment was also equipped with a chaplain, appointed by the Military Board in the case of the first ten regiments of State Troops."

"The Sixth Regiment drilled at Company Shops throughout the month of June, 1861. Much preparation was necessary before the men could take the field. Many problems had to be faced before the regiment could function as an efficient fighting unit. Fisher was still raising troops for his regiment. One company, the Cedar Fork Rifles, came in from Wake County. Another, the Chatham Rifles, came in from Chatham County."

Recruiting

"If you have recd a request from any of our company to make some preparation to take the Ladies of the Cedar Fork Sewing Society to Cary next Wednesday you will please not do so on that day, but any preparation or accommodation shown them on the next Friday to which day the party has been postponed will I assume you be duly appreciated. The sponsoring of social affairs was important to the raising of Confederate troops. It reflected the social temper of the times."

Command

"(Col) Fisher had a problem with William T. Dortch, his lieutenant colonel. Although he was motivated by patriotic fever, Dortch expressed some unwillingness to retain his position with the regiment. On June 1, he wrote Fisher saying that his request for transfer had been denied. Dortch admitted that "matters must remain as they are . . . . I was willing to yield my position, (and am now)." Dortch remained with the regiment for the moment, and even had himself fitted for a uniform towards the end of June. The question of Dortch's position with the regiment would remain temporarily unresolved."

Medical Stores

"As the month of June progressed Fisher continued to face the problems of supplying the regiment with medicines, food, and uniforms. Doctor Nesbitt and his assistants needed many medical supplies to cure the diseases common to rural boys camped together for the first time. From May 15 to June 1 Fisher purchased many medicines from the North Carolina firm of E. W. Hutchison and Company. Among the articles were: "1 vial Sol

Iodid Potash, 1 Bot. Ointment for Recruits, 1 box pills, 5 Bot (s) Salts, 8 oz. Laudanum, 1 Bot. C (Oliver) Oil, 1 tress, 1 vial medicine for Recruits, 2 Bot (s) arrow Root, 3 Prescriptions for Pills for Recruits, etc." Some paregoric, some quinine, and another

prescription completed the list which must have been as distasteful as it was necessary for the men. Fisher expended the sum of $12.80 for this medicine."

Uniform Issues

"More uniform material had to be procured to clothe the growing number of recruits at Camp Alamance. On June 3, Colonel Fisher paid $11.80 for 294 yards of jean material. This material was purchased from F. H. Fries, a local merchant. Many merchants realizing that Colonel Fisher's regiment was a possible "gold mine," solicited the Colonel's business. G. Rosenthal wrote Colonel Fisher from Yanceyville on June 18: 'Captain A. Mitchell told me last week you wanted to buy flannel undershirts & drawers. I have a lot of very good ones, such as our volunteers here (in Caswell Country) received, consisting of about 70 shirts and 50 pr. Drawers, on hand and offer you the same at 75 cts and $1.00 a piece. The quality is as good as can be expected for the price and good many of the shirts sell at $1.25 and $1.50.' Other merchants plagued Colonel Fisher with requests for payment. Kahnweilwe & Bro. a Charlotte clothing firm, wrote Colonel on June 26, requesting payment for "50 pr. Gray blankets" purchased on April 30. This bill involved amounted to $100."

Hired Servants

"I promise to pay Jas. C. Smyth on order One Hundred & Twenty Five dollars for the hire of Randal, who goes with me as a servant into the Campaign in Virginia. I shall clothe & take all care of him under the circumstances—as to health & general safety."

Commissary Stores

"During the month of June Fisher continued to supply food for his men. Early in the month R. W. Griffith was paid $300 for 2,400 pounds of bacon. H. Weatherspoon, Fisher's agent at Cedar Fork, Wake County, wrote: 'I have purchased some 300 lbs. bacon, and I shall be ready to move any time next week, you will please let me know, when you will take us on, and where the company (Co. I., "Cedar Fork Rifles," Capt. R. W. York, comdg.) will respect their bounty.' "

"North Carolina troops, including the Sixth Regiment, had a more varied diet in the early days of the Civil War than is generally supposed. Articles at the Wilmington Railroad Depot, awaiting shipment to troops in Virginia in the Spring of 1861, included bacon, flour, hard bread, beans, rice, coffee, sugar, vinegar, candles, soap, salt, molasses, fish, pickles, dried fruit, corn, cattle lard, and meal. This shows that the average Confederate soldier ate very well, at least in the beginning."

Weapons & Ammunition

"The most important equipment problem faced by the Sixth Regiment was the matter of weapons and military hardware. The equipping of the first ten regiments of State Troops was under the control of the colonel of ordnance for the State of North Carolina. Beginning on May 29 this official issued military equipment to the regiment. On that date Captain Craige of Company G was issued one pair of bullet moulds, one screw driver (for extracting unfired cartridges from muskets), and one clasp. On June 17 the Ordnance Department shipped Fisher 200 rifled muskets, 600 pattern 1822 muskets, 800 barrel wipers, 800 screw drivers, 800 spare cones, 80 spring vises, 80 ball screws, 40 arm chests, 800 cartridges boxes with belts, 800 cap pouches, and 800 bayonet scabbards. On June 28, Fisher received 200 rifled muskets, 200 wipers, 800 screw drivers, 200 spare cones, 20 spring vises, 20 ball screws, and 10 arms chests (for transporting muskets). On June 17, Fisher was furnished with 82 altered muskets which cost the state $600. Company G received 64 blankets, 20 knapsacks, 83 haver sacks, 83 canteens, 84 cartridge boxes, 84 cartridge box belts, 84 belt plates, and 84 bayonet scabbards during the month of June. Another company which might be considered to be representative of the rest of the regiment was Captain Richard Watt York's Company I. These men received 81 cartridge boxes, bayonet scabbards, belts; 81 shirts; 61 coats; 12 pairs of pants; 12 pairs of shoes; 4 camp kettles; 81 knapsacks; and 81 haver sacks during the month of June. While the regiment was at Raleigh, immediately before departing for Virginia the men received 20,000 rifle musket cartridges (with caps), 7,550 musket cartridges, and "12,000 cartridges with caps, recd from Capt. W. W. Pierce."

"**Regiment Colors**"

"In early June Fisher's sister, Christine, presented a fine silken flag to the regiment. The flag, beautifully made of blue silk, carried the state seal, which represented two women standing by a horn of plenty with the words "to be rather than to seem" written below. This was significant motto for the regiment to uphold."

Regimental Life

"For most of the men in the Sixth Regiment life went on at Company Shops, set to the tune of drum beats: the "Troops" for assembling the men in the morning; "Peas-in-a-Trencher, "the beat for breakfast; "Roast Beef," the signal for dinner; the "Surgeon's Call," beat for the men who were sick; the "Assembly," the beat to form the company; the "Color," the signal for formation by battalion; the "Long Roll," the signal for falling in under arms; the "Retreat," to be beat in the evening—for the purpose of reading the orders of the day; the "Tattoo," the signal for "lights out" in the evening."

(This regiment description appeared in "The Bloody Sixth: 6th North Carolina Regiment, CSA (a history) written by Richard W. Iobst and published by the North Carolina Confederate Centennial Commission in Raleigh, NC: 1965; Pages 10-13)

Note: Similar to a modern army unit's "**Table of Organization & Equipment, Infantry Regiment, State Troops, CSA (TO&E or MTO&E).**

APPENDIX "A"

ROSTER OF WD-CSA

Office of the President

His Excellency Jefferson Davis, Commander-in-Chief of the Army-Navy

Colonel Joseph R. Davis, A.D.C. (1861-63)
Colonel G.W. Curtis Lee, A.D.C. (1861)
Colonel Joseph C. Ives, A.D.C. (1861)
Colonel William Preston Johnston, A.D.C. (1861)
Colonel William M. Browne, A.D.C. (1861)
Colonel John Taylor Wood, A.D.C. (1861)
Colonel James Chestnut, Jr., A.D.C. (1861)
Colonel Francis R. Lubbock, A.D.C. (1861)
Colonel John M. Huger, A.D.C. (1861)
Mr. Robert Jesselyn, Military Secretary (Prov.)
Mr. Burton N. Harrison, Military Secretary (Perm.)

General Braxton Bragg. Military Advisor for Operations
Colonel John B. Sale, Bragg's Military Secretary

War Department

Hon. Leroy P. Walker, first Secretary of War
Hon. Judah P. Benjamin, second Secretary of War
Hon. George W. Randolph, third Secretary o War
Hon. James A. Seddon, fourth Secretary of War
Maj. Gen. John C. Breckenridge, fifth Secretary of War
Mr. Albert Taylor Bledsoe, LL.D, Assistant Secretary of War
Hon. John A. Campbell, Judge, Assistant Secretary of War

General Staff

General Samuel Cooper, Adjutant & Inspector General
Chief Clerk
Colonel A. C. Myers, first Quartermaster-General
Brig. Gen. A. R. Lawton, second Quartermaster-General
Colonel L. B. Northrup, first Commissary-General
Brig. Gen. L. M. St. John, second Commissary-General
Brig. Gen. Josiah Gorgas, Chief of Ordnance
Colonel T. S. Rhett, In charge of Ordnance Bureau
Maj. Gen. J. F. Gilmer, Chief of Engineer Bureau

Brig. Gen. S. P. Moore, M.D., Surgeon-General
Brig. Gen. John S. Preston, Chief of the Bureau of Conscription
Colonel T. P. August, Superintendent of the Bureau Conscription
Brig. Gen. John H. Winder, Commanding PC's & Provost Marshal Gen.
Colonel Richard Ould, Chief of the Bureau of Exchange
Colonel Richard Morton, Chief of the Nitre & Mining Bureau
Colonel R. G. H. Kean, Chief of the Bureau of War
Lt. Colonel I. H. Carrington, Assistant Provost Marshal Gen. Richmond
Colonel Thomas I. Bayne, Chief of the Bureau of Foreign Supplies

Courtesy of the D. Appleton Co.

ROSTER OF AAG'S

DEPARTMENT OF WAR
Office of the Adjutant-Inspector General

I.	C.S. A&IG	Samuel Cooper, General	War Dept., Richmond, VA

(NO SEP STAFF for administration: Clerk Pool, War Dept.)

II.	Actg AG	Edward A. Palfrey, Lt.Col.	War Dept., Richmond, VA

Bureau of the A & IG, Appointments Office (1864)

III.	AAG V. D.	Groner, Lt.Col.	War Dept., Richmond, VA
IV.	AA&IG	John Withers, Lt.Col.	(same)
V.	AAG	Jasper S. Whiting, Maj.	(same)
VI.	AAG	George Deas. Maj.	(same)
VII.	AAG	Henry L. Clay, Maj.	(same)
VIII.	AAG	Benjamin S. Ewell, Col.	(same)
IX.	A&IG	Thomas H. Hays, Maj.	(same)
X.	AAG	R. H. Chilton, Maj.	(same)

Bureau of the A & IG

XI.	Signal Corps	William Norris, Maj.	Officer-in-Charge
	1.	J. F. Milligan, Capt.	Columbia, SC

Army Signal Corps (Assigned to the A & IG)

(Also AAG's in Conscription Bureau and Military Prisons Bureau)

** The Consciption Bureau (had AAG assigned)

*** The Bureau of Military Prisons (had AAG assigned)

EASTERN THEATER OPERATIONS

A R M Y L E V E L

A.	AAG	Walter H. Taylor, Lt.Col.	A.N.V.	Camp Lee, Va.
	Mil. Sec.	* commended for meritorious & indefatigable zeal.		
A1.	AAG	Charles S. Venable, Lt.Col.	A.N.V.	(same)
A2.	AAG	Charles Marshall, Lt.Col.	A.N.V.	(same)
A3.	A&IG	H. E. Peyton, Lt.Col.	A.N.V.	(same)
A4.	AA&IG	Giles B. Cooke, Maj.	A.N.V.	(same)
A5.	AAG&JA	H. E. Younger, Maj.	A.N.V.	(same)
A6.	AAG	D. R. Jones	AOP Hqs Beauregard	
A7.	Mil. Sec.	A. L. Long, Col.	A.N.V.	(same)

C O R P S L E V E L

1.	AAG	Gilbert M. Sorrel, Maj.	I Corps	Longstreet's
		* commended for distinguished & gallant service.		
		(later promoted Lt.Col. then Brigadier-General)		
2.	AAG	Charles J. Faulkner, Lt.Col.,	II Corps	Jackson's
3.	AAG	Alexander S. Pendleton, Maj.,	II Corps	Jackson's
4.	AAG	James McHenry Howard, Maj.,	II Corps	Jackson's
		(also AAG, Department of Northern Virginia)		

D I V I S I O N L E V E L

a.	AAG	John W. Daniels, Maj.	Early's Div. I Corps
b.	A&IG	John Marshall Jones, Capt. Magruder's Div.	
		* commended for bravery & efficiency.	
c.	AAG	John Marshall Jones, Maj. Ewell's Div.	
		* commended for bravery & efficiency.	
d.	AAG	John Marshall Jones, Lt.Col. Early's Div.	
		* later Brigadier-General & brigade commander.	
b.	AAG	James McHenry Howard D.H. Hill's Div II Corps	
		* commended meritorious efficiency.	

B R I G A D E L E V E L

(1. AAG Victor Girardey, Capt. Wright's Bde Early's Div. II Corps

(2. AAG Benjamin S. Ewell, Lt.Col. Hood's Bde, Hood's Div I Corps
(2b. AAG William H. Sellers, Lt.Col. (same)
(2c. AAG Paul J. Quattlebaun, Maj. (same)
(2d. AAG Francis L. Price, Capt. (same)
(2e. A&IG John W. Kerr, Capt. (same)

R E G I M E N T A L L E V E L

[a1.	AAG	Richardson Mallett, Jr, 3Lt.	Hall's 46th NC Inf Cook Bde
[a1b.	AAG	Lucio Mitchell, 2Lt.	Hall's (same)
[a1c.	AAG	Robert S. Small, 1Lt. Actg	Hall's (same)
[a1d.	AAG	Thomas Owens, 3Lt. Actg	Hall's (same)
[b1.	AAG	Robert H. Bassett, Capt.	4th TX Inf, Hood's Bde
[b1b.	AAG	William W. Brown, 2Lt.	(same)
[b1c.	AAAG	Frank L. Price, 3Lt.	(same)
[b1d.	AAAG	Jack A. Sutherland, 3Lt.	(same)
[b1e.	AAG	Haywood W. Brahan, 1Lt.	(same)

COMPANY LEVEL

[a1. Orderly Sgt. Joseph H. Freeman, 1SGT Co. "A", 46th NC Inf

[b1. Orderly Sgt. Harry M. Marchant, 1SGT Co. "A", 4th TX Inf

WESTERN THEATER OPERATIONS

A R M Y L E V E L

B.	Chief of Staff	Braxton Bragg, B.Gen.	Dept. West-2 Hqs.
B1.	*Chief of Staff	W.W. Mackall, B.Gen.	A.O.T. Johnston/Bragg
B2.	Chief of Staff	F.A. Shoupe, Col.	A.O.T. Johnston/Hood
B3.	Mil. Sec.	David Urquhart, Col.	A.O.T. Bragg
B4.	AAG	T. B. Roy, Lt.Col.	A.O.T. Camp Bragg, Tn.
B5.	AAG	A. P. Mason, Lt.Col.	A.O.T. (same)
B6.	AAG	Falconer, Lt.Col.	A.O.T. (same)
B7.	AAG	Harrie, Lt.Col.	A.O.T. (same)
B8.	AAG	Henry, Maj.	A.O.T. (same)
B9.	AAG	Clare, Maj.	A.O.T. (same)
B10.	AAG	Benjamin S. Ewell, Lt.Col.	A.O.T. Johnston Hqs
B11.	AAG	H. W. Walter, Maj.	A.O.T. Bragg Hqs
B12.	AAG	George G. Garner, Maj.	A.O.T. (same)

C O R P S L E V E L

1. AG Thomas Jordan, Col., A.O.M., Polk's I Corps
   1b. AAG Douglas West, Maj., A.O.M., Polk's I Corps

2. *Chief of Staff Thomas B. Roy, Col., A.O.T. Hardee's II Corps
   2b. AAG (same) *gallantry, zealous & intelligent
   2c. AAG William D. Pickett, Lt.Col., A.O.T. Hardee's II Corps
   2d. IG Samuel L. Black, Lt.Col., AOT, Hardee's II Corps

3. AAG J. W. Ratchford, Maj., A.O.T. Hood's III Corps

D I V I S I O N L E V E L

a. AAG Archer Anderson, Col., A.O.T. Holmes Div. Hood's Corps

b. AAG W. D. Pickett, Maj. C.A.KY W.J. Hardee's Div

B R I G A D E L E V E L

(1. AAG James E. Hewitt, Capt. 1st KY Bde, Breckenridge Div.
(Confederate civil service—C.S. Post Office Dept.)
* promoted for bravery Maj. & Lt.Col. of 2nd Ky Inf)

R E G I M E N T A L L E V E L

[a1. AAG W. S. Crump 3Lt. 27th MS Regt, Jones Bde
[a1b. AAG G. W. Rice 2Lt. (same)

[b1. AAG Benjamin Jones 2Lt. 3rd MS Regt, Feaherston Bde
[b1b. AAG Junuis Poindexter Lt. (same)
[b1c. AAG Fred S. Hewes Lt. (same)

[c1. AAG R.E. Graves 2Lt. 2nd KY Regt, Hanson Bde
[c1b. AAG Thomas E. Moss, 2Lt. (same)
(refused promotions to stay with 2d KY)

COMPANY LEVEL

[a1c. Orderly Sergeant-R.A. Jarman, 27th MS Inf Regt, Co. "A"
(later promoted to AAG, 2Lt., consolidated Regt.)

[b1c. Orderly Sergeant-Taylor McRae, 3rd MS Inf Regt, Co. "A"

[c1c. Orderly Sergeant-David M. McCutcher, 2nd KY Inf Regt, Co "A"

TRANS-MISSISSIPPI OPERATIONS

A R M Y L E V E L

C. Chief of Staff William B. Boggs, B.Gen., Gen. E.K. Smith Hqs.
C. Chief of Staff Simon B. Buckner, Lt.Gen., (same), Shreveport, LA
C1. A&IG George William Brent, Lt.Col., (same)
C2. AAG Hugh Lawson Clay, Maj., (same)
C3. AAG Paul F. Hammond, Lt., (same)
C4. AAG D. H. Thomson, Capt. (same)
C5. AAG H. P. Pratt, Capt. (same)
C6. AAG S. S. Anderson, Maj. (same)
C7. AAG W. A. Alston, Capt. (same)

C O R P S L E V E L

1. AAG William F. Bullock, Maj., Lt.Gen. R. Taylor's Corps

D I V I S I O N L E V E L

a. AAG D. H. Maury, Capt. Hindmen's Div., non-Corps
a1. AAG Fayette Hewitt, 1Lt. (same) Hqs, Ft. Smith, AR
a2. AAG Samuel W. Melton, 1Lt. (same)
a3. AAAG William Gallaher, 3Lt. (same)
a4. AAAG T. M. Smith, 3Lt. (same)
a5. AAAG R. C. Newton, 3Lt. (same)

b. AAG Thomas L. Snead, Lt.Col.Price's Div., non-Corps
b1. AAG Henry Little, Maj. (same)
b2. AAG James M. Loughborough (Hqs Army of West-Price)
b3. AAG L. A. Mac Lean, Maj. (Hqs, Price's Div)

B R I G A D E L E V E L

(1. AAG Saladin Ridge Watie, 2Lt. 1st Indian Bde, Hindmen's Div
Fort Gibson, IT
(2. AAG C. B. Shepart, Capt. Sibley's 1st TX Bde,
(2a. AAG J. E. Hart, Capt. (same) Ft. Davis, TX
(2b. AAAG W.L. Moore, 3Lt. (same)

(3. Chief of Staff Thomas L. Snead, Col. Price's Hqs MSG
(3b. Adjutant T. B. Wilson, 3Lt. Price's 1st MO Bde, MSG

REGIMENTAL LEVEL

[a1. AAG James Reily, Lt. 4th TX Cav. Regt (Non-Bde)
[a1b. AAG

COMPANY LEVEL

[a1e. Orderly Sergeant Co. "A", 4th TX Cav. Inf Regt

MILITARY DEPARTMENT HEADQUARTERS, C. S.

Department of Northern Virginia, Richmond, VA

1. AAG	James McHenry Howard, Lt.Col.	(Gen. Lee)
1a. AAG	A. P. Mason, Maj.	(Richmond, VA)
1b. AAG	G. M. Bascom, Capt.	(Hqs. Dist. Kawaha)

Department of North Carolina at Raleigh/Wilmington, NC

2. AAG	James G. Martin, B.Gen. AG	(Gen. B. Bragg)
2a. AAG	William Norwood, Maj.	(Kinston)
2b. AAG	R. H. Riddick, Maj.	(Goldsborough)
2c. AAAG	James W. Gordon, Capt.	(same)

Department of Georgia, South Carolina & Florida, Charleston, SC

3. AAG	Charles Stringfellow, Lt.Col.	(Lt.Gen. Hardee)
3a. AG	T. A. Washington, Maj.	(BGen. R. Lee)
3b. AAG	Walter H. Taylor, Capt.	
3c. AAG	J. R. Waddy, Maj.	(Gen. Beauregard)
3d. AAG	Peter Mallett, Maj.	

District Headquarters of East Florida at Tallahassee, FL

31. AAAG	R. B. Thomas, Col.	(MGen. Jones)

Sub-District Headquarters #2 FL at Clear Lake, FL

31a. AAG	W. D. Barnes, 1Lt.	(BGen. Finegame)

Department of Tennessee & SW Virginia, Knoxville, TN

4. AAG	H. S. Bradford, Maj.	(MGen. S. Jones)
4a. AAG	J. F. Belton, Capt.	(same)
4b. AAG	James L. Franser, Lt./ADC	(same)
4c. AAG	Charles S. Stringfellow, Lt.Col.	(same)
4d. AAG	Giles B. Cooke, Maj.	(Chattanooga)

4e. A&IG Merchant, Capt. (same)
4f. AAG H. L. Clay, Maj. (same)
4g. AAG J. G. Martin, Capt. (Aringdon,VA)
4h. AAG G. W. Sorrel, Capt. (Knoxville)

Department of Mississippi, Alabama & East Louisiana, Meridian, MS

5. AAG William F. Bullock, Jr., Lt.Col. (Lt.Gen. Taylor)

Department Trans Mississippi at Shreveport, LA

6. AAG George W. Brent, Lt.Col. (Gen. EK Smith)
6a. AAAG P. B. Leeds, Maj.
6b. AAG George Williamson, Capt.
6c. AAG C. S. West, Capt.
6d. AAG Guy M. Bryan, Maj.
6e. A&IG W. C. Schaumburg, Maj.

District Headquarters, Texas at Houston, TX

61. AAG Edmund P. Turner, Capt. (MGen. J. Magruder's)
61a. AAG Stephen D. Yancy (same)
61b. AAAG C. M. Mason, Capt. (same)
61c. AAG A. H. May, Capt. (Hqs San Antonio)
61d. AAG A. G. Dickerson, LtCol. (Hqs San Antonio)
61e. AAAG E. F. Gray, Maj. (same-SubDist, Rio Grande)
61f. AAAG W. T. Carrington, Lt. (Hqs. Houston)

District Headquarters, Indian Territory at Fort Gibson

62. AAG James Hewitt. Capt. (BGen. A. Pike)
62a. AAG T. M. Scott, Capt. (BGen. Steele)
62b. AAG A. H. Cline, Capt.
62c. AAG J. F. Crosby, Capt.
62d. AAAG B. G. Duval, Lt.

District Headquarters, West Louisiana at Greensburg, LA

63. AAG Eustace Surget, Maj. (Lt.Gen. R. Taylor)

Sub-district Headquarters, East Louisiana at Monroe, LA

63a. AAG	D. F. Boyd, Capt.	DTM (Col. Vincent)

District Headquarters, SW Miss.-East LA, Liberty, MS

64. AAAG	N. T. N. Robinson, Capt.

District Headquarters, Arkansas, Little Rock, AR

65. AAG	Benjamin Allston, Col.
65a. AAG	J. F. Belton, Lt.Col.
65b. AAG	P. H. Thomson, Maj.
65c. AAG	George A. Gallagher, Maj.
65d. AAAG	W. B. Blair, Lt.
65e. AAG	John W. Hinsdale, Capt.

Department of Western Kentucky (#2), Columbus, KY (Defunct)

7. Chief of Staff	John Pegram, Col.	(Hqs. Army of KY)
7a. AAG	William W. Mackey, Lt.Col.	(MGen. L. Polk)
7b. AAG	George G. Garner, Maj.	(same)
7c. A&IG	George W. Brett, Lt.Col.	(same)
7d. AAG	John M. Otey, Maj.	(same)
7e. AAG	George Williams, Maj.	(Hqs. Army of Miss.)
7f. AAG	James Benach, Capt.	(Hqs. Army of KY)
7g. AAAG	H. P. Pratt, Lt.	(same)

STATE MILITARY DEPARTMENTS
(State Troops, Militia's & Home Guards)

1. AG Richard Griffith, B.Gen. — Jackson, Mississippi
    - 1a. A&IG Jones H. Hamilton, BGen.
    - 1b. A&IG W. L. Sykes, BGen.
    - 1c. AAG G. W. Holt, Maj. — (Hqs. MGen. S.D. Lee)
    - 1d. AAG J. L. Cross, Maj. — (Hqs. LtGen. D.H. Hill)
    - 1e. AAG J. R. Waddy, Maj. — (Hqs POW Exchange)

2. A&IG George Goldthwaite, BGen. — Montgomery, Alabama

3. AG Robert A. Toombs, BGen. — Milledgeville, Georgia
    - 3a. A&IG Henry C. Wayne, BGen.
    - 3b. AAG John Dunwody, Maj.
    - 3c. Gustavis W. Smith, MGen. GSM — (same)
    - 3d. Howell Cobb, MGen. GST — (Hqs. Atlanta, GA)

4. A&IG S. R. Gist, BGen. — Columbia, South Carolina
    - 4a. AAG Stephen D. Lee, Capt., SCM
    - 4b. AAG M. L. Bonhan, MGen., SCV
    - 4c. A&IG Wilmut G. De Saussure, BGen.
    - 4d. A&IG Charles H. Simonton, BGen.

5. AG John F. Hoke, Col. Raleigh, — North Carolina
    - 5a. AG James G. Martin, B.Gen.
    - 5b. AG Archer Anderson, BGen.
    - 5c. AAG John C. Winder, Maj.

6. AG Braxton Bragg, Col. LSG — *Baton Rough, Louisiana
    - 6a. AG C. Le D. Elgee, BGen. — Alexandria, LA
    - 6b. A&IG M. Grivot
    - 6c. AAAG Jno G. Devereux, Lt. — New Orleans, LA
    - 6d. P.T.G. Beauregard, Col., LSM
    - 6e. Jolen L. Lewis, MGen., LSM

7. A&IG William T, Austin, BGen. — Austin, Texas
    - 7a. A&IG J. Y. Dashiell, BGen.
    - 7b. AA&IG W. C. Walsh, Col.
    - 7c. A&IG John Burke, BGen.

8. AG Edmond Burgevin, BGen. — Little Rock, Arkansas
8a. AG Gordon N. Peay — Washington, AR

9. AG Daniel Donelson, BGen. — Nashville, Tennessee
9a. AG W. C. Whitthorne, BGen. — (same)

10. AG T. L. Dancy (A&IG), BGen. — Tallahassee, Florida
10a. A&IG Hugh Archer, BGen.
10b. A&IG William H. Milton, BGen.
10c. AG T. W. Brevard, BGen.
10d. R. F. Floyd, FST — Lake City, FL

11. AG George B. Crittenden, BGen. — Frankfort, Kentucky
11a. Simon B. Buckner, BGen. KSG

12. AG Robert S. Garnett, Col. — Richmond, Virginia
12a. AG William H. Richardson

13. AG William Hough, BGen. — Washington, Missouri
13a. Sterling Price, BGen. MSG — Springfield, Missouri

14. Agent Albert Pike, BGen. — Department of Indian Affairs
14a. Steele, BGen. — Fort Gibson, IT

Florida Military Department Staff:

1. AAG W. Call, Lt, Hqs. Tallahassee, FL
2. AAG S. M. Moreno, Lt.
3. AAG William G. Barth, Capt.
   (Also Post AAG, Camp Call, FL)
4. Asst Adjt William Cox

Florida Military Staff CSA:

1. AAG J. M. Galphin, Capt. — Hqs South Florida Forces
2. AAG H. C. Goldthrate, Maj. — Hqs South & East FL
3. AAAG N. Talley, Capt. — Hqs Waldo FL

Tennessee Military Department Staff:

1. AAG Adolphus Heiman, Col.	Hqs. Nashville, TN
2. AAG James W. McHenry, Lt.Col.	
3. AS & AG W. C. Whitthorne, Col.	(same)

Virginia Military Department Staff:

1. AAG Francis H. Smith, Col.	Hqs. Richmond, VA
2. AAG Richard L. Page, Lt.Col.	(same)
3. 3. AAG Walter Taylor, Lt.Col.	Hqs, SF, Richmond, VA

Louisiana Military Department Staff:

AAG David F. Boyd, Capt.	Hqs. Shreveport, LA

Texas Military Department Staff:

1. AAG W. T. Mechling, Capt.	Hqs. Austin, TX
2. AAAG Stephen D. Yancy, Capt.	(same)

Roster Total: 215

The Armies of the Confederate States in the Civil War

The permanent Constitution of the Confederate States of America provided that the President should be commander-in-chief of the army and navy, and of the militia of the several States when called into actual service. Accordingly, in any consideration of the Confederate army, the part played by President Davis must be borne in mind; also the fact that he previously had seen service in the United States army and that he had been Secretary of War of the United States. As Secretaries of War in the Confederate States Government there were associated with President Davis, the following: LeRoy Pope Walker, of Alabama, February 21, 1861, to September 17, 1861 ; Judah P. Benjamin, of Louisiana, September 17, 1861, to March 17, 1862; George W. Randolph, of Virginia, March 17, 1862, to November 17, 1862; Major-General Gustavus W. Smith, of Kentucky, November 17, 1862, to November 21, 1862 ; James A. Seddon, of Virginia, from November 21, 1862, to February 6, 1865 ; and Major-General John C. Breckinridge, of Kentucky, February 6, 1865, to the close of the war. Unlike the Union army there were generals, both regular and of the provisional army, as well as lieutenant-generals ; it being the intention that every commander of an army should rank as general, and every commander of a corps should rank as lieutenant-general. Such was the case with the generals mentioned in the biographical matter following in connection with the various armies and other organizations. An exception to this statement was General Samuel Cooper, who served at Richmond as adjutant and inspector-general.

General Samuel Cooper (U. S. M. A. 1815) was born in Hackensack, New Jersey, June 12, 1798, and served in the army, receiving the brevet of colonel for his services in the Mexican War. He resigned in March, 1861, to enter the service of the Confederacy. He was appointed gene but, owing to his age, took no active part in the field. He was adjutant and inspector-general of the Confederate States army throughout the entire war, performing his duties with great thoroughness and ability. He died at Cameron, Virginia, December 3, 1876.

Army of the Shenandoah
Army of the Peninsula
Army of the Northwest
Army of the Potomac
Army of Northern Virginia
Army of the Kanawha
Army of Eastern Kentucky
Army of New Mexico
Army of Louisiana
Army of Pensacola
Army of Mobile
Central Army of Kentucky
Army of East Tennessee-Army of Kentucky
Army of the Mississippi
Army of Tennessee
Army of Middle Tennessee
Missouri State Guard
Army of the West
Army of West Tennessee-Army of Mississippi
Southern Army - Trans-Mississippi Army
Army of Missouri
Army of Mississippi

Source: "The Photographic History of the Civil War"

This Page last updated 03/29/04

Courtesy of the generalcooper.com

ROSTER OF ADJUTANT GENERAL'S STATE ADJUTANT GENERAL'S DEPARTMENTS Jackson, MISSISSIPPI

1. **TAG Richard Griffith, Brigadier**
2. **A.G. Beverly Matthews**
3. **A.G. William H. Brown**
4. **A.A.G. Isaac N. Davis**
5. **A.A.G. John McGuirk**
6. **A.A.G. F. A. Whiting**
7. **A.A.G. Joseph Bennett**
8. **A.A.G. Livingston Mimms**
9. **A.A.G J. Lewis McManus**
10. **A.A.G. E. D. Frost**
11. **A.A.G. P.S. Layton**
12. **A.A.G. M. R. Clark**
13. **A.A.G. R. C. Miller**

[11]

REGISTER OF COMMISSIONS.

——:o:——

John J. Pettus, Jackson, Commander-in-Chief.
Jefferson Davis, Warren county, Major General, January 23, 1861.
Earl Van Dorn, Claiborne, Major-General.
Charles Clarke, Bolivar, Major-General.
Reuben Davis, Monroe, Major-General.
Earl Van Dorn,, Claiborne, 1st Brigadier-General.
Charles Clarke, Bolivar, 2d Brigadier-General.
James L. Alcorn, Coahoma, 3d Brigadier-General.
C. H. Mott, Marshall, 4th Brigadier-General.
Richard Griffith, Hinds, Brigadier and Adjutant Gen.
William Barksdale, Lowndes, Brigadier-General.
Absalom M. West, Holmes, Brigadier-General.
John M. O'Farrell, Brigadier General.
Charles G. Dalgren, Adams, Brigadier-General.
Beverly Matthews. Lowndes, Adjutant-General.
Wm. H. Brown, Hinds, Adjutant-General.
Samuel G. French, Washington, Chief Ordinance.
Wm. Barksdale, Yazoo, Quartermaster.
Isaac N. Davis, Panola, Assistant-Adjutant-General.
Jehn McGuirk, Marshall County, Asst. A. A. General.
John M. Thompson, Marshall, Quarter-Master General.
Madison McAffee, Holmes, Quartermaster General.
F. A. Whiting, Hinds, Ass't Adjutant-General.
C. R. Dickson, Hinds, Ass't Quarter-Master-General.
Edward Fontaine, Madison, Chief Ordinance.
Joseph Bennett, Rankin, Ass't A. A. General.
Livingston Mimms, Ass't A. A. General.
J. Lewis McManus, Hinds, Ass't A. A. General.
Wm. H. MCardle, Warren, Major.
E. D. Frost, Madison, Asst A. A. General.
P. S. Layton, Rankin, Asst A. A. General.
A. B. Dilworth, Hinds, Asst Quartermaster-General.
James M. Haynes, Asst Quartermaster-General.
M. R. Clark, Asst A. A. General.
W. R. Wood, Asst Quartermaster-General.
R. C. Miller, Ass A. A. General.

Courtesy of the Mississippi State Archives

MISSISSIPPI MILITARY ORGANIZATIONS

serving in the

CIVIL WAR.

Listed by counties

Pensions were granted
March 2, 1888

Laws of Mississippi
1888 - Regular Session
Page 30-

ADAMS COUNTY

12 Inf. Co. B. Natchez Fencibles

16 Inf. Co. D Adams Light Guard
co. 2

16 Inf. Co. I Adams Light Guard
co. 1

Jeff Davis Legion Co. A Adams Troop

10 Inf. Co. B Natchez Southrons

44 Inf. Co. L Tom Weldon Rebels

28 Cav. Co. K Bingaman Rangers

1 Light Artillery, Co. H, Conner Battery

ALCORN COUNTY

41 Inf. Co. I

9 Inf. Co. C Corinth Rifles

Bylthe's Regt. Co. F Capt. Malone

AMITE COUNTY

7 Inf. Co. C Amite Rifles

22 Inf. Co. E Liberty Guards

33 Regt. Inf. Co. K Amite Defenders

33 Inf. Co. B Amite Guards

44 Inf. Co. K. Amite Rangers

4 Cav. Co I Stockdale Rangers

ATTALA COUNTY

13 Inf. Co. I Minute Men of Attala

2 Batt. Inf. (see 48 Inf.) Co. B
Rocky Point Rifles

4 Inf. Co. B Attala Yellow Jackets

4 Inf. Co. I Benela Sharpshooters

4 Inf. Co. K Center Marksmen

15 Inf. Co. A Long Creek Rifles

30 Inf. Co. D Dixie Heroes

40 Inf. Co. D Attala Guards

48 Inf. Co. B Rocky Point Rifles

BENTON COUNTY

2 Inf. Co. B and D

2 Inf. Co. F

34 Inf. Co. B

34 Inf. Co. K

19 Inf.

BOLIVAR COUNTY

1 Cav. Co. H. Bolivar Troops

20 Inf. Co. A McGehee Rifles

28 Cav. Co. E Mayson Dragoons

Capt. Montgomery's Co. Independent Caval

CALHOUN COUNTY

17 Inf. Co. K. Magnolia Guards

42 Inf. Co. F

42 Inf. Co. G Gaston Rifles or (Chickasaw)

4 Inf. Co. F Sons of the South

31 Inf. Co. D Dixie Rebels

19 Batt. Co. B (Cavalry)

2 Miss. Partisan Rangers (Ballentine's Regt. Cavalry) Co. F

CARROLL COUNTY

11 Inf. Co. K Carroll Co. Rifles

42 Inf. Co. A Carroll Fencibles

1 Batt. Sharpshooters Co. A

4 Inf. Co. C Red Invincibles

4 Inf. Co. E Stephen Guards

4 Inf. Co. H Carroll Co. Rebels

15 Inf. Co. B Winona Stars

15 Inf. Co. E McClung Rifles

20 Inf. Co. C Carroll Guards

22 Inf. Co. G Black Hawk Rifles

29 Inf. Co. G Walthall Rebels

30 Inf. Co. A Neill Guards

30 Inf. Co. H Carroll Minute Men

30 Inf. Co. K Dixie Boys

1 Cav. Co. A Carroll Rangers

cont'd

CARROLL COUNTY cont'd

28 Regt. Cav. Co. B Dixie Rangers

2 Miss. Partisan Rangers (Ballentine's Regt. Cav.) Co. A

1 Light Artillery Co. L Vaiden Artillery

6 Batt. Miss. Cav. Capt. Prince Company

CHICKASAW COUNTY

Jeff Davis Legion Co. B Chickasaw Ranger

5 Inf. Co. G Barry Guards

11 Inf. Co. C Prairie Rifles

11 Inf. Co. H Chickasaw Guards

13 Inf. Co. H Spartan Band

17 Inf. Co. A Buena Vista Rifles

24 Inf. Co. C Dowd Rebels

35 Inf. Co. K Invincible Warriors

41 Inf. Co. L Okolona Guards

✓44 Inf. Co. F Palo Alto Guards

11 Cav. Co. H Chickasaw Rangers

12 Cav. Co. F

Blythe's Regt. Cav. Co. F Capt. Malone

2 Regt. Miss. State Cav. Co. B (Johnson Partisans)

24 Inf. Co. H Buena Vista Hornet

COPIAH COUNTY

12 Inf. Co. D Pettus Releif (Rifles)

16 Inf. Co. C Crystal Springs Southern Rights

3 Inf. Co. K McWillie Blues

6 Inf. Co. F Crystal Springs Guards

10 Inf. Co. H Bahala Rifles

36 Inf. Co. A Mount Zion Guards

36 Inf. Co. B Zolliecoffer Avengers

36 Inf. Co. E Hazlehurst Fencibles

36 Inf. Co. G Copiah Rebels

36 Inf. Co. K Dixie Guards

4 Cav. Co. B Copiah Horse Guards

Powers Regt. Cavalry

1 Regt. Inf. State Troops "Minute Men" Co. B

Robert's Co. Miss. Artillery (Seven Stars Art.)

COVINGTON COUNTY

*6 Batt Inf. Co. B Covington Rebels
*Later changed to 46 Reg. Inf.

7 Inf. Co. I Covington Rifles

7 Batt. Inf. Co. G Covington Sharpshooters

27 Inf. Co. F Covington Fencible

2 Inf. Co. D (Quinn's State Troops)

DE SOTO COUNTY

17 Inf. Co. I Pettus Rifles

1 Inf. Co. D DeSoto Grays

9 Inf. Co. A Irrepressibles

9 Inf. Co. E Horn Lake Volunteers

22 Inf. Co. F DeSoto Rebles

29 Inf. Co. I DeSoto Bros.

Wirt Adams Cav. Co. B

18 Batt. Cav. Co. C

18 Batt. Cav. Co. F Pettus Rangers

18 Batt. Cav. Co. K

FORREST COUNTY

FRANKLIN COUNTY

7 Inf. Co. A Franklin Rifles

7 Inf. Co. E Franklin Beuareguards

7 Inf. Co. K Quitman Rifles

33 Inf. Co. D Franklin Guards

4 Cav. Co. I Stockdale Rangers

GEORGE COUNTY

Formed from Jackson & Green Counties

GREENE COUNTY

24 Inf. Co. A Gaines Warriors

3 Batt. Minute Men-State Troops Co. (Greene and Perry County Squad)

GRENADA COUNTY
RMED FROM YALOBUSHA & CARROLL

14 Batt. Light Artillery 1

42 Inf. Co. D

42 Inf. Co. C

42 Inf. Co. H

4 Inf. Co. K Paris Rebels

28 Regt. Cav. Co. A

28 Cav. Co. F

2 Miss. Partisan Rangers (Ballentine's Regt. Cavalry) Co. F

Stanford's Battery-Lt. Artillery

15 Regt. Inf. Co. G Grenada Rifles

Capt. Gage's Co. State Troops Inf. Wigfall Guards

HANCOCK COUNTY

3 Inf. Co. G Gainsville Volunteers

3 Inf. Co. F, H Shieldsboro Rifles

38 Cav. Co. C Hancock Rebels

HARRISON COUNTY

3 Inf. Co. E Biloxi Rifles

3 Inf. Co. F Dahlgren Guards

20 Inf. Co. E Adams Rifles

4 Cav. Co. A

HINDS COUNTY

12 Inf. Co. C Raymond Fencibles

18 Inf. Co. E Miss. College Rifles

18 Inf. Co. H. Brown Rebels

18 Inf. Co. K Burt Rifles

3 Inf. Co. C Dowing Rifles

3 Batt. Inf. Co. K Raymond Minute Mer

22 Inf. Co. B Hinds Right Guards

39 Inf. Co. I Burt Avengers

Powers Reg. Cav.--Owen's Scouts

1 Light Artillery Co. A

3 Regt. Cav. State Troops Co. C

HOLMES COUNTY

12 Inf. Co. F Durant Rifles

1 Batt. Co. B Sharpshooters

4 Inf. Co. C Red Invincibles

4 Inf. Co. G Nelson Grays

15 Inf. Co. C Quitman Rifles

25 Inf. Co. A Red Rebels

38 Regt. Co. A Holmes Volunteers

12 Cav. Co. E

1 Light Artillery Co. I

29 Inf. Co. K

18 Regt. Co. K

3 Inf. Co. G State Troops

HUMPHREYS COUNTY

Formed from Yazoo, Washington, Holmes, Sunflower Counties

ISSAQUENA COUNTY

ITAWAMBA COUNTY

2 Inf. Co. C Town Creek Riflemen

1 Inf. Co. B Moorsville Darts

1 Inf. Co. I Rifle Scouts

1 Inf. Co. K Miss. Yankee Hunters

3 Batt. Inf. Co. B Insurgents

10 Inf. Co. G Fulton Guards

24 Inf. Co. F Cummings Group

41 Inf. Co. I

12 Cav. Co. A

43 Inf. Co. G, Co. H

JACKSON COUNTY

3 Inf. Co. A Live Oak Rifles

27 Inf. Co. L Twigg Rifles

JASPER COUNTY

5 Inf. State Troops Co. B

48 Inf. Co. L Okeibbeha Reserves (p.516)

16 Inf. Co. F

8 Inf. Co. G Jolson Guards

8 Inf. Co. E Tullahoma Hardshells

7 Inf. Co. F Jasper Grays

cont'd

JASPER COUNTY cont'd

27 Inf. Co. I Jasper Rifles

27 Inf. Co. H Jasper Blues

37 Inf. Co. H Jasper Avengers

37 Inf. Co. K Jasper Guards

40 Inf. Co. A Oak Bowery Invincibles

2 Inf. State Troops Co. D

2 Inf. State Troops Co. E

JEFFERSON COUNTY

13 Inf. Co. A Charlie Clark Rifles

19 Inf. Co. D Thomas Hinds Guards

22 Inf. Co. D Rodney Guards

4 Cav. Co. H

Powers Regt. Cav. Owen's Scouts

1 Regt. Light Artillery Co. A

1 Light Artillery Co. K

JEFFERSON DAVIS COUNTY
formed from Lawrence and Covington Coun

28 Cav. Co. E

JONES COUNTY

7 Batt. Inf. Co. B Beauregard Defenders

7 Batt. Inf. Co. F Renovaters

7 Batt. Inf. Co. C Jones Co. Rebels

8 Inf. Co. K Ellisville Invincibles

27 Inf. Co. B Rosin Heels

3 Batt. Cav. Co. E (Capt. Gillis' Co.)

KEMPER COUNTY

13 Inf. Co. C Kemper Legion

Jefferson Davis Legion Co. C Southern Guards

5 Inf. Co. I Kemper Rebles

6 Batt. Inf. Co. K Kemper Guards

24 Inf. State Troops Co. I Kemper Rebels

2 Cav. Co. H Kemper Dragons

11 Cav. Perrin's Co. (A?)

Gamblin's Cav. State Troops

35 Inf. Co. A

LAFAYETTE COUNTY

11 Inf. Co. A University Greys

11 Inf. Co. G Lamar Rifles

19 Inf. Co. E McClung Rifles

19 Inf. Co. F Avant Southrons

1 Regt. Inf. Co. G Dave Rogers Rifles

9 Inf. Co. H. Lafayette Guards

22 Inf. Co. H. Lafayette Farmers

22 Inf. Co. K Pegins Defenders

29 Inf. Co. A Lafayette Rebels

34 Inf. Co. C Smith Rifles

1 Cav. Co. B Thompson Cavalry

2 Miss. Partisan Rangers (Ballentine's Regt. Cav.) Co. G

41 Inf. Co. H ("C")

17 Inf. Co. K Magnolia Guards

cont'd

LAFAYETTE COUNTY cont'd

3 Regt. Alcorn's Brig. Co. G, 2nd Regt. (State Troops Ida Invincibles)

3 Cav. Co. I

4 Inf. Co. D Paris Rebels

LAUDERDALE COUNTY

13 Inf. Co. E Alumutcha Inf.

13 Inf. Co. F Lauderdale Zowaves

13 Inf. Co. K Pettus Guards

5 Inf. Co. C Lauderdale Spring Greys

6 Batt. Inf. Co. F Lauderdale Rifles

8 Inf. Co. E Tullahoma Hardshells

8 Inf. Co. H Southern Sentinels

8 Inf. Co. I Confederate Guards

14 Inf. Co. H Meridian Invincibles

27 Inf. Co. H. Jasper Blues

36 Inf. Co. C Harper Reserves

36 Inf. Co. H Edwards Tigers

37 Inf. Co. A Pattons Company

37 Inf. Co. I McLemore Guards

41 Inf. Co. C Cole Gurads

2 Cav. Co. C Lauderdale Cavalry

5 Regt. Inf. Co. C

LAMAR COUNTY

Formed from Marion and Pearl River Countie

LAWRENCE COUNTY

12 Inf. Co. K Lawrence Rifles

7 Inf. Co. G Goode Rifles

22 Inf. Co. A Miss. Greys

33 Inf. Co. C Johnson Guards

14 Batt. Artillery Brookhaven Light Artillery July 21, 1861

LEAKE COUNTY

6 Inf. Co. C Quitman Southerner

27 Inf. Co. E Leake Guards

33 Inf. Co. F Leake Rebels

Wirt Adams Cav. Co. D

15 Miss. Batt. Co. C Capt. James M. Graham

40 Inf. Co. G Capt. Latimer

40 Inf. Co. B Capt. Yates

LEE COUNTY

2 Inf. Co. E Calhoun Rifles

17 Inf. Co. C Quitman Greys

41 Inf. Co. K

41 Inf. Co. I

19 Inf. Co. K Jake Thompson Guards

2 Cav. Co. E Moorsville Blues

LEFLORE COUNTY

Formed from Sunflower, Carroll and Tallahatchie Counties

LINCOLN COUNTY

12 Inf. Co. K Lawrence Rifles

27 Inf. Co. C Fredonia Hards

27 Inf. Co. D Rayburn Rifles

27 Inf. Co. I Harris Rebels

21 Inf. Co. C Stevens Rifles

14 Batt. Artillery Brookhaven Light Artillery

LOWNDES COUNTY

10 Inf. Co. D Lowndes Southrons

10 Inf. Co. E Southern Avengers

11 Inf. Co. E Prairie Guards

14 Inf. Co. K Columbus Riflemen

24 Inf. Co. D Calendonia Rifles

35 Inf. Co. C Capt. Jordan

35 Inf. Co. F Capt. Gregory

35 Inf. Co. H. Confederate Vols.

35 Inf. Co. K Invincible Warrior

43 Inf. Co. B Capt. J. M. Billeys

43 Inf. Co. F Capt. Hampton

43 Inf. Co. I Capt. J. O. Banks

44 Inf. Co. A Tombigbee Rangers

48 Inf. Co. C Blewett's Company

6 Cav. Co. H

6 Cav. Co. I

6 Cav. Co. K

8 Cav. Co. E (19 Batt.) /4 Batt. Cav. Co.(

cont'd

LOWNDES COUNTY cont'd

8 Cav. (19 Batt.) Co. F Capt. Field

8 Cav. (19 Batt.) Co. G Capt. Matthews

11 Cav. Co. H Capt. Battle Fort

10 Regt. 12 Batt. Cav. Co. C

12 Miss. Cav. (16 Confed.) Co. F Capt. Moore

3 Batt. Co. A Lowndes Co. Minute Men

1 Regt. Co. G of Artesia Captain Hardy

MADISON COUNTY

18 Inf. Co. C Confederates

18 Inf. Co. G Camden Rifles

18 Inf. Co. I Beauregard Rifles

21 Inf. Co. G

10 Inf. Co. I Madison Rifles

24 Inf. Co. E Helen Johnson Guards

Wirt Adams Cav. Co. D

Partisan Rangers Kelly Co.

Madison Light Artillery

Madison Rifles

Wirt Adams Cav. Co. M

1 Regt. Minute Men Co. F Inf.

MARION COUNTY

7 Inf. Co. D Jeff Davis Sharpshooters

7 Inf. Co. F Marion's Men

MARSHALL COUNTY

17 Inf. Co. B Miss. Rangers

17 Inf. Co. F Sam Benton Relief Rifles

17 Inf. Co. G Confederate Guards

19 Inf. Co. I

1 Regt. Inf. Co. A Walker Reserves

1 Regt. Inf. Co. F Alcorn Rifles

9 Inf. Co. B Home Guards

9 Inf. Co. D Jeff Davis Rifles

9 Inf. Co. F Quitman Rifle Guard

34 Inf. Co. E Coldwater Rebels

34 Inf. Co. F Goodman Guards

34 Inf. Co. I Bowen Rifles

44 Inf. Co. H Pettus Rangers

12 Cav. Co. F

18 Batt. Cav. Co. C

2 Miss. Partisan Rangers (Ballentine's Reg Cav.) Co. F, H

34 Inf. Co. D Wynne's Relief

LOWNDES COUNTY cont'd

8 Cav. (19 Batt.) Co. F Capt. Field

8 Cav. (19 Batt.) Co. G Capt. Matthews

11 Cav. Co. H Capt. Battle Fort

10 Regt. 12 Batt. Cav. Co. C

12 Miss. Cav. (16 Confed.) Co. F Capt. Moore

3 Batt. Co. A Lowndes Co. Minute Men

1 Regt. Co. G of Artesia Captain Hardy

MADISON COUNTY

18 Inf. Co. C Confederates

18 Inf. Co. G Camden Rifles

18 Inf. Co. I Beauregard Rifles

21 Inf. Co. G

10 Inf. Co. I Madison Rifles

24 Inf. Co. E Helen Johnson Guards

Wirt Adams Cav. Co. D

Partisan Rangers Kelly Co.

Madison Light Artillery

Madison Rifles

Wirt Adams Cav. Co. M

1 Regt. Minute Men Co. F Inf.

MARION COUNTY

7 Inf. Co. D Jeff Davis Sharpshooters

7 Inf. Co. F Marion's Men

MARSHALL COUNTY

17 Inf. Co. B Miss. Rangers

17 Inf. Co. F Sam Benton Relief Rifles

17 Inf. Co. G Confederate Guards

19 Inf. Co. I

1 Regt. Inf. Co. A Walker Reserves

1 Regt. Inf. Co. F Alcorn Rifles

9 Inf. Co. B Home Guards

9 Inf. Co. D Jeff Davis Rifles

9 Inf. Co. F Quitman Rifle Guard

34 Inf. Co. E Coldwater Rebels

34 Inf. Co. F Goodman Guards

34 Inf. Co. I Bowen Rifles

44 Inf. Co. H Pettus Rangers

12 Cav. Co. F

18 Batt. Cav. Co. C

2 Miss. Partisan Rangers (Ballentine's Reg Cav.) Co. F, H

34 Inf. Co. D Wynne's Relief

SHARKEY COUNTY

Formed from Issaquena, Washington and Warren (?)

SIMPSON COUNTY

16 Inf. Co. B Westville Guards

6 Inf. Co. H Invincibles

39 Inf. Co. A Greys

39 Inf. Co. F Pearl River Guards

1 Batt. Co. E Minute Men

SMITH COUNTY

16 Inf. Co. H Defenders

6 Inf. Co. D Lowery Rifles

6 Batt. Inf. Co. G Singleton Guards

6 Batt. Inf. Co. H Raleigh Rangers

8 Inf. Co. A Yankee Terrors

8 Inf. Co. C True Confederates

36 Inf. Co. C Harper Reserves

37 Inf. Co. G Yancey Guards

46 Inf. Co. H, Co. G

37 Inf. Co. H

1 Cav. Reserves Co. B

STONE COUNTY

Formed from Harrison, Perry & Jackson (?)

SUNFLOWER COUNTY

21 Inf. Co. I Guards

3 Inf. Co. B Dispersers

TALLAHATCHIE COUNTY

21 Inf. Co. F Rifles

32 Reg. Co. E Hatchie Tigers

1i Cav. Tallahatchie Guards

TATE COUNTY

Formed from DeSoto, Marshall & Tunica

42 Inf. Co. B Senatobia Guards

Wirt Adams Cav. Co. B

2 Cav. Co. D Senatobia Opposers

18 Batt. Co. H Peach Creek Avengers

TIPPAH COUNTY

2 Inf. Co. L Liberty Guards

2 Inf. Co. B O'Conner Rifles

2 Inf. Co. D Joe Matthews' Rifles

2 Inf. Co. F Magnolia Rifles

19 Inf. Co. H Salem Cav.

3 Batt. Inf. Co. F Highlanders

23 Inf. Co. B Falkner Guards

23 Inf. Co. C Tigers

23 Inf. Co. E Thompson Invincibles

23 Inf. Co. G Tippah Rifle Co.

23 Inf. Co. H Mobino Rifles

23 Inf. Co. K Stubbs Rifles

34 Inf. Co. A Rangers

34 Inf. Co. B Rebels

34 Inf. Co. G Sons of Liberty

cont'd

TIPPAH COUNTY cont'd

34 Inf. Co. K Dixie Guards

2 Miss. Cav. Co. E Partisan Rangers (Ballentine's Cavalry)

2 Inf. Army of 10,000 Co. C

TISHOMINGO COUNTY

2 Inf. Co. A Riflemen

2 Inf. Co. K Iuka Rifles

17 Inf. Co. E Burnsville Blues

26 Inf. Co. C Davenport Grays

26 Inf. Co. E Wince Price Guards

26 Inf. Co. D (Iuka)

26 Inf. Co. F Anna Perry Guards

26 Inf. Co. G (Iuka)

26 Inf. Co. H (Iuka)

1 Inf. Co. H James Creek Vols.

9 Inf. Co. C Corinth Rifles

23 Inf. Co. A Blount Guards

23 Inf. Co. D Kossuth Vols.

23 Inf. Co. F Blackland Gideonites

32 Reg. Co. K Buckner Boys

32 Reg. Co. A Revengers

32 Reg. Co. G Lowery Invincibles

32 Reg. Co. C Rebels

43 Inf. Co. K

2 Miss. Partisan Rangers (Ballentine's Reg. Cav.) Co. F

TUNICA COUNTY

UNION COUNTY

Formed from Pontotoc & Tippah

21 Inf. Co. K New Albany Group

WALTHALL COUNTY

Formed from Pike and Marion

WARREN COUNTY

12 Inf. Co. G Vicksburg Sharpshooter

19 Inf. Co. C Warren Rifles

21 Inf. Co. A Volunteer Southrons

21 Inf. Co. H Volunteers

21 Inf. Co. L. Confeds

6 Batt. Inf. Co. E Rebels

10 Inf. Co. F Hill City Cadets

22 Inf. Co. C Sarsfield Southrons

24 Inf. Co. G Briarfield Defenders

Wirt Adams Cavalry, Co. F (First Mississippi Cavalry)

28 Cav. Co. C. Buckner's Light Horse

28 Cav. Co. I Johnson Rebels

48 Inf. (2nd Batt.) Co. E

48 Inf. Co. G Manlone's Co.

48 Inf. Co. H Vicksburg Volunteers

Warren Light Artillery p. 880

1st Miss. Light Artillery Co. G

WASHINGTON COUNTY

22 Inf. Co. I Swamp Rangers

28 Cav. Co. D

WAYNE COUNTY

13 Inf. Co. B Wayne Rifles

6 Batt. Inf. Co. A Gaines Invincibles

14 Cav. Co. E

5 Regt. Co. H Minute Men

State Troops Reserve

2 Regt. Co. B

WEBSTER COUNTY

Formed from Choctaw, Montgomery, Chickasaw, and Okitebbeha

3 Regt. Inf. Minute Men Co. H, I

WILKINSON COUNTY

16 Inf. Co. K Rifles

21 Inf. Co. D Jeff Davis Guards

21 Inf. Co. E Hurricane Rifles

38 Cav. Co. D Guards

4 Cav. Co. I Stockdale Rangers

WINSTON COUNTY

13 Inf. Co. A Guards

5 Inf. Co. D New Prospect Grays

5 Inf. Co. E Pettus Rebels

5 Inf. Co. F Rifles

14 Inf. Co. F Beaugard Rifles

cont'd

WINSTON COUNTY cont'd

20 Inf. Co. G Barksdale Greys

11 Cav. Co. D Mitts Compsny

35 Inf. Co. A, I, D

1 Inf. Army of 10,000

1 Inf. Co. I State Troops

13 Inf. Co. F

11 (Perrin's Cavalry) Co. D

23 Regt. Co. I

YALOBUSHA COUNTY

2 Batt. Inf. (48th) Dixie Boys

15 Inf. Co. F Water Valley Rifle Guards

15 Inf. Co. G Grenada Rifles

15 Inf. Co. H Yalobusha Rifles

29 Inf. Co. D, E

44 Inf. Co. E Blythe Rifles

18 Batt. Cav. Co. C

19 Batt. Co. C Duff Guards

2 Miss. Partisan Rangers, Co. I (Ballentine Regt. Cav.)

3 Regt. Cav. Co. F Barksdale Rangers

YAZOO COUNTY

12 Inf. Co. I Sartartia Rifles

18 Inf. Co. B Benton Rifles

18 Inf. Co. D Homer Rifles

18 Inf. Co. F McClung Rifles

3 Inf. Co. I Sharp's Co.

6 Batt. Inf. Co. C Pickets

6 Batt. Inf. Co. E Jeff Davis Rebels

10 Inf. Co. K Minute Rifles

29 Inf. Co. H Gale Reserves

30 Inf. Co. E Greys

Wirt Adams Regt. Cav. Co. A

Wirt Adams Regt. Co. K, Cav.

18 Batt. Cav. Co. A

46 Regt. Co. E

1 Regt. Artillery Co. I

1 Regt. Artillery Co. B Vaughan Rebels

Confederate States Army Military Publications

C.S.A. FIELD MANUAL REFERENCES

1.	W.H. Hardee	Infantry Tactics,Vol 1 & 2, 1858
2.	S. Cooper	Soldiers Manual, 1861
3.	S. Cooper	Uniforms & Insignia of the CSA, 1862
4.	Dr. De Leon	Surgeon's Manual, 1861
5.	Chaplain's Assn	A Confederate Soldier's Prayer Guide, 1861
6.	S. Cooper	Infantry Tactics, 1852
7.		The Code of Military Justice
8.		Saber Manual
9.		Artillery Manual

Rank	Collar insignia	Sleeve insignia	Buttons
General	(all grades)	(all grades)	
Lieutenant General			LtGen: Groups of three buttons
Major General			MajGen: Groups of three buttons
Brigadier General			BrigGen: Groups of two buttons

Joseph Reid Anderson in a CSA brigadier general's uniform

1500659R

HD. QRS. ARMY OF NORTHERN VA.
October 31, 1863.

GENERAL ORDERS,
No. 96

It frequently happens that enlisted men, who are detailed to perform light duty, on surgeon's certificate of disability for active service, fail to report as directed. It is ordered, therefore, that in future all men so detailed will be assembled at such time and point as shall be indicated by their respective corps commanders, and sent to the provost marshal at the nearest rail road station, who will see that they proceed and report as their orders require.

By command of General R. E. LEE.

W. H. TAYLOR,
A. A. General.

Courtesy of the National Archives

Head Qrs Walthall's Brigade
Hindman's Div. Hood's Corps Army Tenn
Near Dalton Georgia
March [illegible]

Special Orders
No 20

The following named Officer having been elected & having passed a satisfactory examination pursuant to existing orders is hereby announced.

Pvt S. H. [illegible] to be 2d Lt Co F 27th Miss Regt Elected 8th March 1864 to fill vacancy caused by the acceptance of the Resignation of 2d Lt H. J. [illegible]

He will be obeyed & respected accordingly.

By Command of
Lt Col R. P. McKelvaine
J. C. Harrison
A. A. A. G.

Courtesy of the National Archives

15106 60R

HEAD QRS. ARMY NORTHERN VA.
March 30, 1864.

GENERAL ORDERS, }
No. 23. }

In compliance with the recommendation of the Senate and House of Representatives, his Excellency the President of the Confederate States has issued his proclamation, calling upon the people to set apart Friday the 8th of April as a day of humiliation, fasting and prayer.

The Commanding General invites the army to join in the observance of the day. He directs due preparations to be made in all departments to anticipate the wants of the several commands, so that it may be strictly observed. All military duties, except such as are absolutely necessary, will be suspended. The Chaplains are desired to hold divine service in their regiments and brigades. The officers and men are requested to attend.

Soldiers! Let us humble ourselves before the Lord our God, asking, through Christ, the forgiveness of our sins, beseeching the aid of the God of our forefathers in the defence of our homes and our liberties, thanking him for his past blessings, and imploring their continuance upon our cause and our people.

R. E. LEE, *General.*

Courtesy of the National Archives

HEAD QUARTERS ARMY OF NORTHERN VA.,
19th April, 1864.

GENERAL ORDERS, }
No. 32. }

I. In all cases of discharge properly claimed under Par. VIII, General Order No. 42, Adjt. & Insp'r Genl's Office, current series, the commanding officer of a regiment or battalion to which the applicant belongs will make out and forward to these Head Quarters, through the proper channel of communication, and three days before the date of the expiration of the soldier's term of enlistment, the "Soldier's Discharge" for the approval of the General Commanding, without which no discharge will be considered complete. The Regimental commander will state in the discharge the exact age of the applicant, that he has not re-enlisted and that the description given therein is a true transcript from the Muster Roll of the company.

II. Under authority of the Hon. Secretary of War, candles will be issued, by the Commissary Department upon the requisition of commanding officers, certifying that the same are necessary for the proper performance of official business in their respective offices and that no candles have been drawn from the Government for the time specified as follows:

To Corps Head Quarters, - - - -	10 pounds per month.
" Division " - - -	7 " " "
" Brigade " - - -	4 " " "
" Regimt'l " - - -	3 " " "

IN ADDITION TO THE ABOVE THERE WILL BE ISSUED:

To Corps and Division Quarter Masters, -	5 pounds per month
" Brigade and Regimental " " -	4 " " "
" Post Quarter Masters, - - -	8 " " "
" Depot Commissaries, - - -	8 " " "
" All other, - - - - -	4 " " "

The Quarter Master and Commissary in each case to make the requisition and to give the certificate required above.

III. The General Commanding directs the following modifications of paragraph II, General Orders No. 37, from these Head Quarters. The Chief Quarter Master of the Army will see that they are carried into effect without delay:

There will be allowed for the Head Quarters of each Division,	one six (6) horse wagon.
For transportation of Medical stores of every two battalions of artillery,	one two (2) " "
For the Chief Quarter Master and C. S. of the Artillery of the Army—one four (4) horse wagon. For the Chief Quarter Master and C. S. of the Artillery of each Corps,—one four (4) horse wagon.	These wagons will also be required to transport the forage for the animals at the Head Quarters respectively.

For the officers of each regiment including Field, Staff, Surgeon, Quarter Master, C. S. and company officers,—one four (4) horse wagon. For the officer of a battalion of artillery including Field, Staff, Surgeon, Quarter Master and company officers,—one four (4) horse wagon.

By command of Gen'l R. E. Lee.

W. H. TAYLOR,
A. A. General.

Courtesy of the National Archives

HD. QRS. DEPARTMENT NORTHERN VA.
May 2, 1864.

GENERAL ORDERS, }
No. 37. }

I. Continuation of the proceedings of a General Court Martial, convened at the Camp of Early's Division, by virtue of Special Orders, No. 8, Head Quarters Department of Northern Virginia, current series, before which were arraigned and tried the following prisoners—(The Specifications are omitted):

1.—Lieut. J. M. DUNAWAY, Company E, 31st Ga. Regiment.

CHARGE—Absence without leave.

FINDING.

Of Specification,	Guilty.
Of Charge,	Guilty.

SENTENCE.

And the Court do therefore sentence him Lieutenant J. M. Dunaway of the thirty-first Georgia Regiment, to forfeit one month's pay, and to be publicly reprimanded by his brigade commander.

2.—Private JOHN GAY, Company G, 38th Ga. Regiment.

CHARGE—Absence without leave.

PLEA.

To Specification,	Guilty.
To Charge,	Guilty.

FINDING.

The Court confirm the pleas of the accused, and are satisfied that the accused was unable for duty because of sickness for at least a portion of his absence, and is of good general character.

SENTENCE.

The Court do therefore sentence him Private John Gay of Company G, of the thirty-eighth Georgia Regiment, when not on regular duty, to do fatigue duty, when practicable, for three months, and besides that, for the time he was absent without leave, to forfeit his pay for the same period.

3.—Lieutenant GEORGE R. WELLS, Company D, 38th Ga. Regiment.

CHARGE—Absence without leave.

PLEA.

To Specification,	Guilty.
To Charge,	Guilty.

FINDING.

The Court confirm the pleas of the accused.

Courtesy of the National Archives

HEAD QRS. ARMY OF NORTHERN VA.
July 20, 1864.

GENERAL ORDERS, }
No. 50. }

Colonel W. H. STEVENS, P. A. C. S., is announced as Chief Engineer of this Army, and will be respected accordingly.

By command of General R. E. LEE.

W. H. TAYLOR,
A. A. General.

Courtesy of the National Archives

No. 78.

Confederate Roll of Honor.

GENERAL ORDERS, No. 64. | ADJT. AND INSP. GENERAL'S OFFICE, *Richmond, Va., August* 10, 1864.

I. The following roll of honor is published, in accordance with paragraph I, General Orders, No. 131, 1863. It will be read to every regiment in the service at the first dress-parade after its receipt.

* * * * * * *

BATTLE OF JENKINS' FERRY.

MISSOURI.

Eighth Regiment of Infantry.

Capt. E. A. Pinnell, Co. D.
Capt. A. M. Curry, Co. G.
First Lieut. T. L. Johnson, Co. C.
Senior Second Lieut. James Hulsey, Co. E.
Junior Second Lieut. M. O. Roberts, Co. F.
Junior Second Lieut. T. B. Logan, Co. I.

Ninth Regiment of Infantry.

Private George E. Kirby, Company G.

Tenth Regiment of Infantry.

Private A. J. Hutchison, Co. E.
Private Ozias Denton, Co. F.
Private J. R. Adams, Co. G.
Private Stephen Crismon, Co. K.

Eleventh Regiment of Infantry.

Private W. H. Dodson,* Co. A.
Private Peter Black,* Co. B.
Private D. O. Daugherty, Co. C.
Private William Park, Co. D.
Sergt. Green B. Smith,* Co. F.
Private B. F. Mock, Co. G.
Private Thomas Conner,* Co. H.
Private Jacob S. Barnard,* Co. I.
Sergt. S. B. McBride, Co. K.

Company E on detached service.

Twelfth Regiment of Infantry.

Private J. W. Kilgore, Co. A.
Sergt. James Hawkins, Co. B.
Private H. K. Taylor, Co. C.
Sergt. George Hirsch, Co. D.
Private John E. Morris, Co. E.
Sergt. James Lincycomb, Co. F.
Private M. Gibson, Co. G.
Sergt. William Kemp, Co. H.
Sergt. A. J. Hinkle, Co. I.
Private N. C. Foster, Co. K.

Sixteenth Regiment of Infantry.

Private Loyed T. Stephenson,* Co. C.
Private D. P. Neel,* Co. F.
Private William Tyree, Co. I.
Private W. L. Jackson, Co. K.

Other companies declined selecting.

Ninth Battalion of Sharpshooters.

Private W. B. McElwee, Co. A.
Sergt. H. B. Stiles, Co. B.
Private W. Clay Green, Co. C.
Private John King, Co. D.

Lesueur's Battery.

Corpl. Jefferson H. Gillespie.

By order:

S. COOPER,
Adjutant and Inspector General.

---

* Killed in action.

a matter of surprise that with my handful of men I was unable to prevent the construction of the dams at the falls of Red River by the enemy, since the large forces on the other side likewise failed to prevent that construction with equal if not greater opportunities.

The troops under my command behaved, with few exceptions, better than I expected under the impressions received from Colonel Harrison's representations. I may be allowed, however, to select for special commendation and respectfully to recommend to the attention of the general commanding Lieut. Col. F. W. Moore and Capts. R. Sewell and H. P. Wells, of Harrison's regiment; Major Waddill, of McNeill's regiment, and Capt. W. H. Corbin, of Capers' regiment, all of whom were conspicuous for gallantry. Lieutenant-Colonel Moore is competent to fill a much higher position than he now occupies. I am grateful to my staff for their faithful and efficient discharge of their respective duties.

I am, colonel, respectfully, your obedient servant,

ST. JOHN R. LIDDELL,
Brig. Gen., Provisional Army Confederate States.

Lieut. Col. GEORGE WILLIAMSON,
Assistant Adjutant-General, Trans-Mississippi Dept.

No. 106.

Confederate Roll of Honor.

GENERAL ORDERS, No. 64. } ADJT. AND INSP. GENERAL'S OFFICE, *Richmond, Va., August* 10, 1864.

I. The following Roll of Honor is published in accordance with paragraph I, General Orders, No. 131, 1863. It will be read to every regiment in the service at the first dress parade after its receipt:

* * * * * * *

BATTLE OF PLEASANT HILL.

MISSOURI.

Eighth Regiment of Infantry.

Capt. William Dings, Co. C.
First Lieut. James T. Otey, Co. A.
First Lieut. Josiah Rodgers, Co. K.
Senior Second Lieut. W. P. Thomas, Co. B.
Senior Second Lieut. William H. Frazier, Co. K.
Junior Second Lieut. J. W. Rogers, Co. H.

Ninth Regiment of Infantry.

First Sergt. Thompson Fry, Co. E.
Private James Wood Co. I.

Tenth Regiment of Infantry.

Private A. J. Hutchison, Co. E.
Private Ozias Denton, Co. F.
Sergt. James F. Hollinsworth, Co. G.
Sergt. James C. Dyer, Co. K.

Head Quarters Military Post,

AMERICUS, GA. Sept. 24th, 1864.

ORDERS—No 1.

I. By order of General Hood Commanding the Army and Department of Tennessee ,I assume command of the Post of Americus Georgia.

II. All officers on duty at this Post, will report in writing to these Head Quarters, by what authority they are on duty, giving the number and date of the order of assignment: they will also report the names of detailed men, Clerks, and citizens in their employ, or under their command, giving the date of contract, or the No. and date of the Orders of detail.

The reports of Surgeons in charge of Hospitals, made thro the Senior Surgeon of the Post, will embrace, in addition to the above, the name, No and date of Orders of each Surgeon and assistant Surgeon, the name and date of contract of each contract Physician, the name and date of appointment of each Hospital Steward, and the No. and Rank of all patients in Hospital.

A similar report will be made, at the close of each month hereafter, showing the alterations, that have taken place since last report.

III. All men at or in the vicinity of this Post who hold special details or exemptions to follow Mechanical, Agricultural, or professional pursuits, will report in person at these Head Quarters and exhibit their detail or exemption papers.

BARNA B. BLUE,
Capt, 3rd Confederate Regt, Infantry,
Commanding Post.

Courtesy of the National Archives

HEAD QUARTERS CONFEDERATE ARMY,
9th. February, 1865.

GENERAL ORDER, }
No. 1. }

In obedience to General Order No. 3, Adjutant & Inspector General's Office, 6th February, 1865, I assume command of the Military forces of the Confederate States. Deeply impressed with the difficulties and responsibility of the position and humbly invoking the guidance of Almighty God, I rely for success upon the courage and fortitude of the Army, sustained by the patriotism and firmness of the people, confident that their united efforts, under the blessing of Heaven, will secure peace and independence.

The Head Quarters of the Army, to which all special reports and communications will be addressed, will be for the present with the Army of Northern Virginia. The stated and regular returns and reports of each Army and Department will be forwarded as heretofore to the Office of the Adjutant & Inspector General.

R. E. LEE,
General.

90710
AF
Oct. 14. 1891

C.S.A. 160
13

Crandall
645
(no. 1)

Courtesy of the National Archives

HEAD QUARTERS ARMIES OF THE CONFEDERATE STATES,
11th *February*, 1865.

GENERAL ORDERS,
No. 2.

In entering upon the campaign about to open, the General-in-Chief feels assured that the soldiers who have so long and so nobly borne the hardships and dangers of the war, require no exortation to respond to the calls of honor and duty.

With the liberty transmitted by their forefathers they have inherited the spirit to defend it.

The choice between war and abject submission is before them.

To such a proposal, brave men with arms in their hands can have but one answer.

They cannot barter manhood for peace nor the right of self government for life or property.

But justice to them requires a sterner admonition to those who have abandoned their comrades in the hour of peril.

A last opportunity is afforded them to wipe out the disgrace and escape the punishment of their crimes.

By authority of the President of the Confederate States a pardon is announced to such deserters and men improperly absent as shall return to the commands to which they belong within the shortest possible time, not exceeding twenty days from the publication of this Order, at the Head Quarters of the Department in which they may be.

Those who may be prevented by interruption of communications, may report within the time specified to the nearest enrolling officer or other officer on duty, to be forwarded as soon as practicable, and upon presenting a certificate from such officer showing compliance with the requirement, will receive the pardon hereby offered.

Those who have deserted to the service of the enemy, or who have deserted after having been once pardoned for the same offence, and those who shall desert or absent themselves without authority after the publication of this Order, are excluded from its benefits. Nor does the offer of pardon extend to other offences than desertion and absence without permission.

By the same authority it is also declared that no general amnesty will again be granted, and those who refuse to accept the pardon now offered, or who shall hereafter desert or absent themselves without leave, shall suffer such punishment as the Courts may impose, and no application for clemency will be entertained.

Courtesy of the National Archives

HEAD QUARTERS ARMIES OF THE CONFEDERATE STATES,
22nd *February*, 1865.

GENERAL ORDERS,
No. 4.

I. The experience of our own and other armies having established, that the safety no less than the efficiency of troops, requires that order be maintained, and every man kept in his proper position in action, the following instructions will be immediately carried into effect:

A thorough examination by competent officers selected by the Corps Commander, or officer commanding detached troops, will be made as to the qualifications and character of the commissioned and non-commissioned officers of each company. Such of the former as shall be reported deficient in intelligence, coolness, and capacity, will be brought before Examining Boards, and those of the latter so reported, will be reduced to the ranks. Appointments to fill vacancies among the non-commissioned officers will be made from those soldiers of the company most distinguished for courage, discipline and attention to duty. The whole number of file closers in each company shall be one for every ten men, and for this purpose Lance appointments will be given if necessary, to men of the character above described, who will be required to wear a distinctive badge.

II. The file closers, will be carefully instructed in their duties by the regimental commanders, and vacancies will be filled as they occur among the non-commissioned and Lance officers from the best and most tried soldiers of the company. On the march they will be required to prevent straggling, and be held responsible for the presence of their respective squads of ten. In action, they will keep two paces behind the rear rank of their several squads, the non-commissioned and Lance officers with loaded guns and fixed bayonets. They will be diligently instructed to aid in preserving order in the ranks and enforcing obedience to commands, and to permit no man to leave his place, unless wounded, excused in writing by the Medical officer of the regiment, or by order of the regimental commander. For this purpose, they will use such degree of force as may be necessary. If any refuse to advance, disobey orders, or leave the ranks to plunder or to retreat, the file closers will promptly cut down or fire upon the delinquents. They will treat in the same manner any man who uses words or actions calculated to produce alarm among the troops. Justice to the brave men who remain at their posts, no less than the success to our arms, demands that this order be rigorously executed, and it will be enjoined upon file closers that they shall make the evasion of duty more dangerous than its performance.

APPENDIX "C"

RECORD of [illegible]

from the 19th *day of* [illegible] 1861 *to the* [illegible] *day of* [illegible] 1865

Roster of Commissioned Officers.

☞ In the following *Roster*, begin with the highest official rank in the organization, and record together the names of all who have filled a particular position, in the order of their succession, then record each inferior rank in similar manner. Some names will therefore be repeated as occurring in different official positions. **Include these names also in the Record on opposite page, in the first rank they held in the original organization.**

No.	NAMES.	RANK.	APPOINTMENT.		COMMISSION EXPIRED.	
			DATE OF.	AUTHORITY OF.	WHEN.	CAUSE.

Courtesy of the National Archives

from the State of Mississippi in the service of the Confede[rate]

186 , (date of organization) to the ______ day of ______ 186

ENGAGEMENTS.	Present and Absent accounted for	REMARKS.

☞ Herein show accurately all *dates*, as of elections, promotion[s], resignations, deaths, transfers, desertions, discharges, retireme[nt], capture, exchange or escape, or took oath to the United Stat[es]. Mention meritorious or dishonorable facts, and character of seri[ous] and disabling wounds, and when and where received. N[ote] "substitutes," and for whom received. Note also, "re enlist[ed] men" under Act of December 11th, 1861, or those held [in] service by Act of April 16th, 1862, and where and from wh[at] organization.

Record of [illegible]

States of America in the war with the [illegible] States, from the [illegible] day of [illegible]

☞ Under "ENGAGEMENTS," head the column with name [illegible] ere the engagement lasted more than one day, take a column for each day; d use the following characters to mean—P Present and un[illegible] w. Severely wounded; k. Killed; a. Absent without leave; a. f. Absent furlough or satisfactorily; a. d. Absent on detail or duty by [illegible] sick; a w. Absent wounded; a. c. Absent captured; a. a. Absent under rest; c. Captured; X. Deserted; m. Missing; p. d. Present [illegible] Mortally wounded. Those marked thus (*) in column of names, re-enlisted ider Act of December 11th, 1861, or were held in service by Act of April 16th, 1862.

No.	NAMES, ☞ Insert the name of every officer and enlisted man who has been connected with the organization, and show under "Remarks" what has been the fate of each one. Give first name in full.	Rank.	ENLISTED.			BORN. (State.)	Occupation.	RESIDENCE. (Nearest P. O.)	Age when enlisted.	Married or single. (M. or S.)
			When.	Where.	Period.					

HISTORICAL MEMORANDA.

☞ Make such succinct narrative of organization and service, as of Stations, Marches, Battles, incidents, &c., as may be necessary for perfect record, being particular as to dates.

ADVANCE AND RETREAT.

"*Strength of the Army of Tennessee, on the 31st of July, 1864;* [illegible] *September, 1864; 6th November, 1864; and 10th December, 186*[illegible]

July 31st, 1864.

	PRESENT.			ABSENT.	
	Effective.	Total.	Aggregate.	Total.	Aggr[illegible]
Infantry................	30,451	39,414	43,448	93,759	101,[illegible]
Cavalry..............	10,269	15,904	17,313	26,354	28[illegible]
Artillery..............	3,775	4,610	4,840	6,317	6[illegible]
Total Army...........	44,495	59,928	65,601	126,430	136[illegible]

September 20th, 1864.

	PRESENT.			ABSENT.	
	Effective.	Total.	Aggregate.	Total.	Agg[illegible]
Infantry..............	27,094	36,301	39,962	81,824	8[illegible]
Cavalry..............	10,543	15,978	17,416	27,005	2[illegible]
Artillery..............	2,766	3,408	3,570	4,628	[illegible]
Total Army...........	40,403	55,687	60,948	113,457	12[illegible]

November 6th, 1864.

	PRESENT.			ABSENT.	
	Effective.	Total.	Aggregate.	Total.	Agg[illegible]
Infantry..............	25,889	34,559	38,119	79,997	87[illegible]
Cavalry..............	2,306	3,258	3,532	4,778	5[illegible]
Artillery..............	2,405	2,913	3,068	4,018	4[illegible]
Total Army...........	30,600	40,730	44,719	88,793	96[illegible]

COMPARISON OF LOSSES.

December 10th, 1864.

	PRESENT.			ABSENT.	
	Effective.	Total.	Aggregate.	Total.	Aggregate.
[illegible]ry..............	18,342	27,222	29,826	71,329	77,631
[illegible]ry..............	2,306	3,258	3,532	4,778	5,148
[illegible]ry..............	2,405	2,913	3,068	4,018	4,203
[illegible]l Army..........	23,053	33,393	36,426	80,125	86,982

"Respectfully submitted,

"A. P. MASON,

"Lieutenant Colonel, A. A. G."

" COLUMBUS, GEORGIA, *April 3d, 1866.*

onsolidated summaries in the Armies of Tennessee and Mississippi g the campaign commencing May 7th, 1864, at Dalton, Georgia, nding after the engagement with the enemy at Jonesboro' and the ation of Atlanta, furnished for the information of General J. E. on.

solidated summary of casualties of the Armies of Tennessee and Mississippi in the series of engagements around and from Dalton, Georgia, to the Etowah river, for the period commencing May the th, and ending May 20th, 1864:

CORPS.	Killed.	Wounded.	Total.
ee's	119	859	978
's..............................	283	1,564	1,847
s Army, Mississippi......	42	405	447
	444	2,828	3,372

should be remembered that, in all estimates of the strength of Armies, mber of *effectives* is alone to be considered; therefore, the first column, in regoing return, is that to which reference should be made. Also, that of ty thousand four hundred and three (40,403) effectives reported present for n the 20th September, forty-five hundred (4500) cavalry were absent with der, in Tennessee. This latter circumstance accounts for my statement, uently, that we had thirty-five thousand (35,000) effectives during the

APPENDIX "D"

LIST OF DOCUMENTS

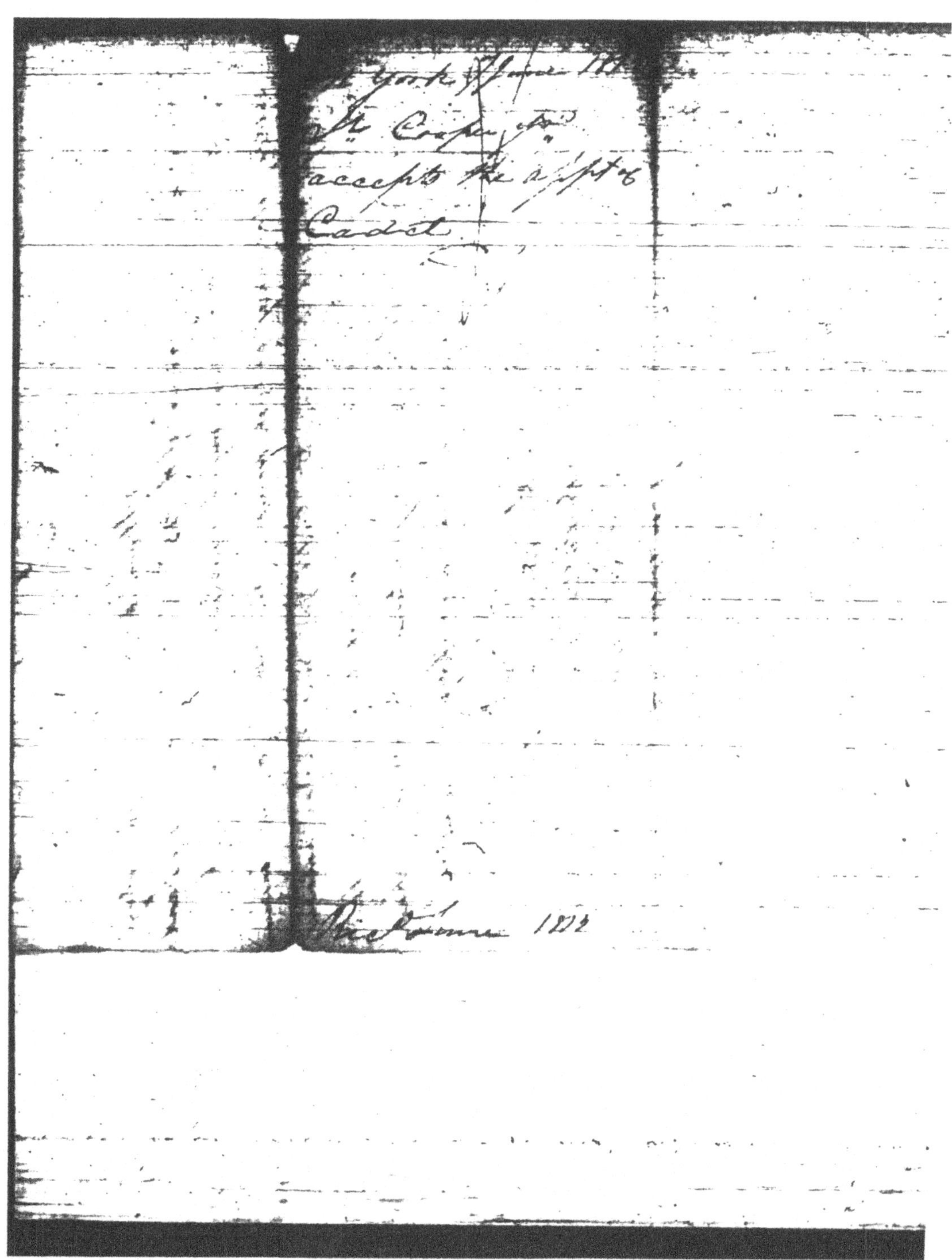

Courtesy of the National Archives

EIGHTH

ANNUAL REUNION

OF THE

Association of the Graduates

OF THE

United States Military Academy,

AT

WEST POINT, NEW YORK,

JUNE 14, 1877.

New York:
A. S. BARNES & CO.
111 & 113 WILLIAM STREET.
1877.

SAMUEL COOPER.

No. 156. CLASS OF 1815.

Died December 14, 1876, at Cameron, Va., aged 81.

GENERAL COOPER was admitted as a Cadet from the State of New York, May 25, 1813, and was graduated December 11, 1815. For a record of his long life and service I have been disappointed in obtaining a sketch of his life from those who were most intimate with him, and shall therefore confine this brief notice to that contained in General Cullum's Biographical Register. On date of graduation he was appointed a Brevet Second Lieutenant of Light Artillery. He served in garrison at New England posts from 1815 to 1818, then in the Adjutant-General's office until 1825; again in garrison in Florida till the following year, when he was ordered to the Artillery School at Fort Monroe for two years. He served as Aide-de-Camp to Major-General Macomb from 1828 to 1836, and on Staff duty at headquarters of the Army from 1836 to 1841.

He became Captain of the 4th Artillery June 11, 1836, and Brevet Major Staff Assistant Adjutant-General July 7, 1838. He served in the Florida war as Chief of Staff of Colonel Worth, 1841 and 1842, being engaged against the Seminole Indians. From 1842 until 1852 he was on special duty in the War Department, with the rank of Lieutenant-Colonel and Assistant Adjutant-General from March 3, 1847. He was brevetted Colonel, May 30, 1848, for meritorious conduct, particularly in the performance of his duties in the prosecution of the war with Mexico. He became Adjutant-General of the Army with the rank of Colonel, July 15, 1852, and continued in charge of the Adjutant-General's office at Washington until March 7, 1861, when he resigned. He afterwards became the Adjutant-General of the Confederate Army. In 1836 he published "A concise system of instructions and regulations for the Militia and Volunteers of the United States." After the close of the war in 1865 he resided at Cameron, near Alexandria, Va., where he died.

(*Secretary of the Association.*)

REGISTER

OF THE

GRADUATES OF THE U. S. MILITARY ACADEMY,

FROM ITS ESTABLISHMENT MARCH 16, 1802,
TO JANUARY 1, 1890.

was subsequently brevetted for his gallantry to a Lieutenant-Colonelcy. After the Mexican War his life was not particularly eventful, except a short revival of his wilderness experience when he commanded the Gila Expedition of 1857.

Having attained the rank of Colonel, and from age and exposure in the line of duty becoming disqualified for active service, he was retired, Sept. 9, 1861, and hence did not take the field during the Civil War, though he continued to perform valuable and responsible duties, for which, at its close, he was brevetted a Brigadier-General, in recognition of his "long and faithful services in the army" of half a century.

Though the remainder of his days was chiefly taken up with his private affairs, he always felt a lively interest in all matters pertaining to the development of the Great West, particularly the progress of railroad enterprises through the regions he was among the first to penetrate with wagons, and by the pathways in which he always claimed to have been the pioneer to subsequent explorers. Though he seldom spoke of his remarkable exploits, he devoted his leisure hours to arranging his maps and collecting his notes, with a view of leaving behind much important information omitted by Washington Irving, to whom any allusion in connection with his adventures was displeasing.

Aside from the high qualities of bravery, enterprise, and pertinacity of purpose which so eminently fitted him to become the great explorer of our Western wilds, he was noted for his amiable qualities of head and heart. His cheerful manner and *débonnaire* appearance will long be remembered by all, young and old, who had the pleasure of his acquaintance. After the fitful fever of a long and active life, Death, the mighty archer, has at last taken him to the happy hunting grounds, the blissful abode of kindred souls.

"Of no distemper, of no blast he died,
But fell like autumn fruit that mellow'd long;
Even wonder'd at, because he dropt no sooner.
Fate seem'd to wind him up for fourscore years;
Yet freshly ran he on five winters more,
Till, like a clock worn out with eating time,
The wheels of weary life at last stood still."

156...(Born N. Y.)....**SAMUEL COOPER**..........(Ap'd N. Y.)

Military History. — Cadet of the Military Academy, May 25, 1813, to Dec. 11, 1815, when he was graduated and promoted in the Army to

BVT. SECOND LIEUT., LIGHT ARTILLERY, DEC. 11, 1815.

Served: in garrison at New England Posts, 1815–18; in the Adjutant-

(SECOND LIEUT., LIGHT ARTILLERY, NOV. 15, 1817)

General's Office, at Washington, D. C., 1818–25; in garrison at Ft.

(SECOND LIEUT., 1ST ARTILLERY, IN RE-ORGANIZATION OF ARMY, JUNE 1, 1821)

(FIRST LIEUT., 2D ARTILLERY, JULY 6, 1821)

(TRANSFERRED TO 4TH ARTILLERY, DEC. 31, 1824)

Marion, Fla., 1825–26, — Ft. Monroe, Va. (Artillery School for Practice), 1826–28, — and Ft. Columbus, N. Y., 1828; as Aide-de-Camp to Major-

(BVT. CAPT., JULY 6, 1831, FOR FAITHFUL SERVICE TEN YEARS IN ONE GRADE)

General Macomb (General-in-Chief), May 29, 1828, to June 11, 1836; on

(CAPTAIN, 4TH ARTILLERY, JUNE 11, 1836, TO JULY 15, 1852)

(BVT. MAJOR, STAFF — ASST. ADJUTANT-GENERAL, JULY 7, 1838)

Staff duty, at headquarters of the Army, 1836–41; in the Florida War,

as Chief of Staff of Colonel Worth, June 28, 1841, to Aug. 17, 1842, being engaged against the Seminole Indians, in the Rout of Halleck Tustennuggee's Band in the Big Hammock of Pilaklikaha, Apr. 19, 1842;

(LIEUT.-COLONEL, STAFF — ASST. ADJUTANT-GENERAL, MAR. 3, 1847)

(BVT. COLONEL, MAY 30, 1848, FOR MERITORIOUS CONDUCT, PARTICULARLY IN THE PERFORMANCE OF HIS DUTIES IN THE PROSECUTION OF THE WAR WITH MEXICO)

on Special duty in the War Department, 1842–52; and in charge of the

(COL., STAFF — ADJUTANT-GENERAL OF THE U. S. ARMY, JULY 15, 1852)

Adjutant-General's Office at Washington, D. C., July 26, 1852, to Mar. 7, 1861.

RESIGNED, MARCH 7, 1861.

Civil History. — Compiler of "A Concise System of Instructions and Regulations for the Militia and Volunteers of the United States," 1836.

Joined in the Rebellion of 1861–66 against the United States.

Civil History. — Farmer, near Alexandria, Va., 1866–76.

DIED, DEC. 14, 1876, AT CAMERON, FAIRFAX CO., VA.: AGED 81.

157....(Born Ct.)....**CHARLES DAVIES**..........(Ap'd N. Y.)

Military History. — Cadet of the Military Academy, Dec. 27, 1813, to Dec. 11, 1815, when he was graduated and promoted in the Army to

BVT. SECOND LIEUT., LIGHT ARTILLERY, DEC. 11, 1815.

Served: in garrison at New England Posts, 1815–16; at the Military

(TRANSFERRED, AS SECOND LIEUT., TO CORPS OF ENGINEERS, AUG. 31, 1816)

(RESIGNED, FROM CORPS OF ENGINEERS, DEC. 1, 1816)

Academy, 1816–37, as Principal Asst. Professor of Mathematics, Dec. 1, 1816, to Oct. 31, 1821, and of Natural and Experimental Philosophy,

(PROFESSOR OF MATHEMATICS, MILITARY ACADEMY, MAY 1, 1823)

Oct. 31, 1821, to May 1, 1823, — and Professor of Mathematics, May 1, 1823, to May 31, 1837.

RESIGNED, MAY 31, 1837.

Civil History. — Professor of Mathematics, Trinity College, Hartford, Ct., 1839 to 1841. Member of the Board of Visitors to the Military Academy, 1841.

Military History. — Re-appointed in the Army with the rank of

MAJOR, STAFF — PAYMASTER, U. S. ARMY, NOV. 17, 1841,

and served as Paymaster at West Point, N. Y., 1841–45, and Treasurer of the Military Academy, Dec. 11, 1841, to Dec. 19, 1846.

RESIGNED, SEP. 30, 1845.

Civil History. — Professor of Mathematics and Philosophy, University of New York, Sep., 1848, to July, 1849. President of the Teachers' Association of the State of New York, Aug. 2, 1843, to Aug. 2, 1844. Professor of Higher Mathematics, Columbia College, New York city, May 18, 1857, to June, 1865, and Emeritus Professor, 1865–76. Author of a complete series of Mathematical Text-Books, 1837–67, embracing "Primary Arithmetic and Table-Book;" "First Lessons in Arithmetic;" "Intellectual Arithmetic;" "New School Arithmetic," with "Key;" "Grammar of Arithmetic;" "New University Arithme-

GENERAL SAMUEL COOPER

(June 12, 1798- Dec. 3,1876)

Adjutant and Inspector General of the Confederate States of America

This letter by Ex-President Jefferson Davis appeared in the Southern Historical Society Papers, Volume III, January to June, 1877.

Letter from President Davis

Mississippi City, Mississippi, April 5th, 1877.

General F. Lee:

My Dear Sir-I am gratified to know that you have under-taken to make a record of the services and virtues of a man than whom none has higher claims upon the regard of all who loved the Confederacy. No one presents an example more worth of the emulation of the youth of his country. My personal acquaintance with General Cooper began at the time when he was associated with Mr. Poinsett in the War Office, where his professional knowledge was made available to the Secretary, in those army details of which a civilian was necessarily but little informed. His sterling character and uniform courtesy soon attracted the attention and caused him to be frequently resorted to by members of Congress having business with the War Office. Ex-President Pierce, who was then a Senator, spoke in after years of the favorable impression which General Cooper had made upon him, and said his habit had been when he "wanted information to go to Cooper instead of to the Secretary;" But while he thus bought to the service of the Secretary his professional knowledge, the latter eminently great in other departments of learning, no doubt did much to imbue General Cooper's mind with those political ideas which subsequently marked him as more profoundly informed upon the character of our Government than most others of his profession.

In the midst of his professional duties, he found leisure for high literary culture, had much dramatic taste, and in the dull days of garrison life he contributed much to refined enjoyment. When I became Secretary of Ward, General Cooper was Adjutant-General of the United States army. My intercourse with him was daily, and as well because of the purity of his character as his knowledge of the officers and affairs of the army, I habitually consulted him in reference to the duties I had to perform.

Though calm in his manner and charitable in his feelings, he was a man of great native force, and had a supreme scorn for all that was mean.

To such a man, a life spent in the army could not fail to have had its antagonisms and its friendships; yet when officers were to be selected for special duties, to be appointed in staff corps, or to be promoted into new regiments, where qualifications were alone to be regarded, I never, in four years of constant consultation, saw Cooper manifest prejudice, or knew him to seek favors for a friend, or to withhold what was just from one to whom he bore reverse relations. This rare virtue-this supremacy of judgment over feeling-impressed me as being so exceptional, that I have often mentioned it as a thing so singular and so praiseworthy that it deserves to be known by all men.

When in 1861 a part of the Southern States, in the exercise of their sovereignty, passed ordinances of secession from the Union, and organized a separate Confederacy, General Cooper was at the head of the corps, in which a large part of his life had been passed. This office was one for which he was peculiarly qualified, and which was best suited to his taste. He was a native of a Northern State; his sole personal relation with the South was that he was the husband of a granddaughter of George Mason, of Virginia-Virginia, not yet belonging to the Confederate States. He foresaw the storm, which was soon to burst upon the seceding States-saw that the power which had been refused in the convention which formed the Constitution of the Union-the poser to use the military arm of the General Government to coerce a State, was to be employed without doubt, and conscientiously believing that would be violative of the fundamental principles of the compact of Union, he resigned his commission, which was his whole wealth, and repaired to Montgomery to tender his services to the weaker party, because it was the party of law and right.

The Confederate Government had no military organization, and, save the patriotic hearts of gallant men, had little on which to rely for the defense of their country. The experience and special knowledge of General Cooper was, under these circumstances, of incalculable value. If he would consent, while his juniors led armies in the field, to devote himself to the little attractive labors of the Adjutant-General's office-if he would consent? They little knew the self-sacrificing, duty-loving nature of Cooper, who did not anticipate his modest request "to be employed wherever it was thought he might be useful," and with unrelaxing assiduity he applied himself to the labors of the Adjutant-General's office. The many who measure the value of an officer's service by the conspicuous part he played upon the fields of battle, may not properly estimate the worth of Cooper's services in the war between the States, but those who like yourself were in a position to know what he did, what he prevented, what he directed, will not fail to place him among those who contributed most to whatever was achieved.

Faithful to the cause he espoused-unmoved by the prospect of disaster, when the fortune of war seemed everywhere to be against us-Cooper continued unswerving in the discharge of his duty, and when the evacuation of the capital became a necessity, he took with him such books and papers as were indispensable, and although worn down by incessant labor, never relaxed his attention to the functions of his office until disease compelled him to confess his inability to continue the retreat. The affection, the honor and the confidence with which I regarded him made our parting a sorrowful one, under circumstances so had for us both. Of the events which followed his return to the spot where his house had stood, you are so well informed that I will not protract this already long letter.

I remain with great regard and affectionate remembrance,

Yours,

Jefferson Davis

[Home Page][General Fitzhugh Lee's Comments] [Early Life Of Cooper] [Email]

◂ Back

Confederate States of America,

WAR DEPARTMENT,

Richmond, October 1st 1863.

Sir:

You are hereby informed that the President has appointed you

Brigadier General,

In the Provisional Army in the service of the Confederate States: to rank as such from the thirtieth day of September one thousand eight hundred and sixty three. Should the Senate, at their next session, advise and consent thereto, you will be commissioned accordingly.

Immediately on receipt hereof please to communicate to this Department, through the Adjutant and Inspector General's Office, your acceptance or non-acceptance of said appointment; and with your letter of acceptance, return to the Adjutant and Inspector General the OATH, herewith enclosed, properly filled up, SUBSCRIBED and ATTESTED, reporting at the same time your AGE, RESIDENCE when appointed, and the STATE in which you were BORN.

[illegible] duty to General Bragg

James A. Seddon

Secretary of War.

Courtesy of the National Archives

COOPER

GENERALS AND LIEUTENANT GENERALS CONFEDERATE STATE ARMY IN ORDER OF RANK.

	Name.	State.	Date of rank.	Remarks.
	GENERALS.			
1	Saml. Cooper	Va.	May 16, 1861	Adjutant General.
2	A. S. Johnston	Tex.	May 30, 1861	Killed at Shiloh, Tenn., Ap 6, 1862.
3	Robert E. Lee	Va.	June 14, 1861	Genl. in chief, Jan. 31, 1865.
4	Jos. E. Johnston	Va.	July 4, 1861	
5	P. G. T. Beauregard	La.	July 21, 1861	
6	Braxton Bragg	La.	April 12, 1862	
	GENERAL PROVISIONAL ARMY.			
1	E. Kirby Smith	Fla.	Feb. 19, 1864	
	GENERAL WITH TEMPORARY RANK.			
1	Jno. B. Hood	Tex.	July 18, 1864	
	LIEUTENANT GENERALS.			
1	Jas. Longstreet	Ala	Oct. 9, 1862	
2	E. Kirby Smith	Fla	Oct. 9, 1862	See list of Generals.
3	Leonidas Polk	La	Oct. 10, 1862	Killed at Pine Mountain, G June 14, 1864.
4	T. H. Holmes	N. C.	Oct. 10, 1862	
5	Wm. J. Hardee	Ga	Oct. 10, 1862	
6	Thos. J. Jackson	Va	Oct. 10, 1862	Killed at Chancellorsvil Va., May 10, 1863.
7	Jno. C. Pemberton	do	Oct. 10, 1862	
8	Richd. S. Ewell	do	May 24, 1863	
9	A. P. Hill	do	May 24, 1863	Killed at Petersburg, V April 2, 1865.
0	Jno. B. Hood	Tex	Sept. 20, 1863	See list of Generals.
1	Richd. Taylor	La	April 8, 1864	
12	Jubal A. Early	Va	May 31, 1864	
13	R. H. Anderson	S. C.	May 31, 1864	
14	S. D. Lee	S. C.	June 23, 1864	
15	A. P. Stewart	Tenn.	June 23, 1864	
16	S. B. Buckner	Ky.	Sept. 20, 1864	
17	Wade Hampton	S. C.	Feb. 14, 1865	
18	N. B. Forrest	Tenn.	Feb. 28, 1865	
• 19	Jno. B. Gordon	Ga		Notified of appointment commission not issued.
20	Jos. Wheeler	Ala		

Courtesy of the United Daughters of the Confederacy

ARMY OF THE CONFEDERATE STATES.

CERTIFICATE OF DISABILITY FOR DISCHARGE.

(To be used, in duplicate, in all cases of discharge on account of disability.)

Richard Meosons Prevost, of Captain McLemore Company, (B,) of the 27th Miss Regiment of Confederate States Vol, was enlisted by Capt McLemore of the 27th Regiment of Miss Vol at Ellisville Miss on the 10th day of August 1861, to serve three years; he was born in St Clair Co in the State of Alabama, is 22 years of age, 6 feet, — inches high, fair complexion, Blue eyes, light hair, and by occupation when enlisted a Farmer. During the last two months said soldier has been unfit for duty 60 days. (Here consult directions on Form Med. Dept. Gen. Reg.)

STATION: Rome Geo

DATE: April 14th 1863 S. V. D. Hill act Surgn in Chg Bell Hospital

I CERTIFY, that I have carefully examined the said Richd Meosons of Captain McLemore's Company, and find him incapable of performing the duties of a soldier because of (Here consult par. 1134, p. 244, and directions on Form 13, p. 260, Med. Dept. Gen. Reg.) Chronic Diarrhoea He is unfit for duty. Has not been on duty [illegible]

Wm C Nichols,
Lewis C Pynchon, Surgeon
Exmg Board

DISCHARGED this 14th day of April, 1863, at Rome Geo

A H Caldwell Col Commanding the Post.

NOTE 1.—When a probable case for pension, special care must be taken to state the degree of disability.
NOTE 2.—The place where the soldier desires to be addressed may be here added.

* Town— Marion County Lauderdale State— Miss

(DUPLICATES.)

Courtesy of the National Archives

DECEASED SOLDIERS' CLAIMS.

INSTRUCTIONS AND FORMS.

I. The pay and allowances due to any deceased officer or enlisted man, is paid first, to the widow of the deceased if living, and if not, to the children, if any; and in default of widow or children, to the father, if living, and if not, to the mother of the deceased.

II. If the child or children be minor, payment will be made the guardian, upon the production of the proper certificate of guardianship, under the seal of the Court.

III. The claimant must produce his or her affidavit, and that of one disinterested witness, stating the relationship. For instance, if the claimant be a mother, the affidavit must state that there is living neither wife, child, nor father of the deceased; if the father, that there is neither wife nor child; and if the child, that there is no widow. The magistrate, or other proper officer, must testify to the credibility of the witness, and the Clerk of the Court must certify, under the seal of the same, that he is such magistrate.

IV. When there is an administrator, a certificate of the fact by the proper officer of the Court granting the same, under his seal of office, will be all that is necessary.

V. If, within their knowledge, claimants should state *where* the officer or soldier *was born*, and *when* and *from what cause he died*, distinguishing those who were *killed in battle*, or *died of wounds received in battle*, from those *who died of disease*.

VI. When they can do so, claimants will name the captains and companies to which deceased belonged; also at what place and when they entered the service. They should always endorse on their papers, in plain writing, their *address*, naming *post office, County and State*.

VII. These instructions are substantially those adopted by the Second Auditor, and must be strictly complied with. Claims prepared as herein directed, should be forwarded to my address. After being recorded, they are transmitted for settlement to Col. W. H. S. TAYLOR, Second Auditor, at Richmond.

VIII. Where claimants have been furnished by Company officers with the final statements of their deceased relatives, they should forward such statement with the claim; and it being essential to the perfection of a history of Mississippi Troops, now in course of preparation, they are requested to furnish the undersigned with the full christian and surname of deceased, his age when enlisted, the town or county and State of his birth, when and where he first entered the service, and the town or county of which he was a resident when enlisted; also, if known, in what actions he may have participated; if wounded, on what occasion and how; date and cause of death, etc.

IX. The form of Power of Attorney may be used or not as the party may elect. In either case, the claim will be duly forwarded, and will be attended to as promptly as the business of the Second Auditor will allow, and the amounts found due will be remitted to the parties entitled as they may direct. Where parties prefer constituting me their attorney, I will collect the amount and forward to their address, making no charge for my services—the State having made ample provision in that respect.

All communications should be addressed to

MAJ. J. L. POWER,

Superintendent Army Records, Mississippi Troops, Jackson Miss.

Courtesy of the National Archives

Richmond Va
July 28. 63

It gives me pleasure to to bear testimony to Col Halls eminent qualifications for promotion and I recommend it earnestly

Jno R Cooke
Brig Genl

Respectfully Submitted to the President -

There are vacant N. C Brigades and unless pre-ponderating qualifications are presented by other officers, I recommend Col Hall's promotion

7th Augt 63
J. A. Seddon
Sec of War

Secty of War, please have the examination suggested made so that it may be known whether there are other candidates of higher qualifications
J. D.

Gov. Z. B. Vance 134.
of No. Ca. N.C.
[illegible]
Raleigh, N. C.
July 24, 1863.

North Carolina

Strongly recommending for promotion Col. Edward D. Hall, Cooke's Brigade, who is also recommended by Genl. Cooke & has received recommendations from other sources

Secty of War, for attention
J. D.
Secy of War
Recd July 29/63

A. G.
Report the N C Brigades now wanting Brigadiers & if in Gen Lee's army, if any special recommendations of Brigadiers for them have been made by him
J. A. S.
Sec
15th Augt 63

Respectfully Submitted to the Secy of War. The brigade formerly commanded by Genl Pettigrew is the only N. C brigade now wanting a brigadier. Col. W. W. Kirkland is recommended by Genl Lee for the command of this brigade & the papers are now before the Hon Secy of War.

A. & I. G. O.
Aug 27/63
Ed A Palfrey
Lt Col & A. A. G.

Secy of War

A. G.
Col Kirkland has been appointed to Pettigrew's Brigade
J. A. S.
Sec
28th Augt 63

Courtesy of the National Archives

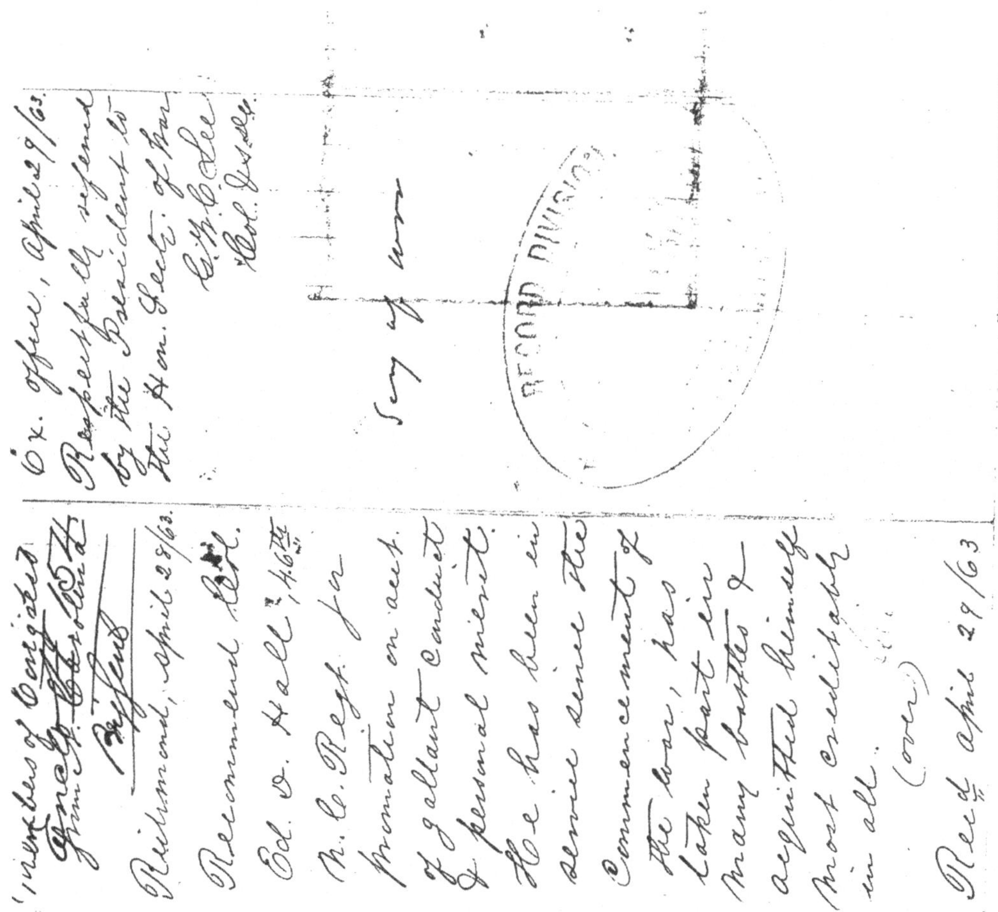
Members of Congress
from N. Carolina
Present

Richmond, April 28/63.

Recommend [illegible].

Col. O. Hall, 46th
N. C. Regt. for
promotion on acct.
of gallant conduct
& personal merit.
He has been in
service since the
commencement of
the war, has
taken part in
many battles &
acquitted himself
most creditably
in all.

(over)

Recd. April 29/63

Ex. Office, April 29/63.
Respectfully referred
by the President to
the Hon. Secty. of War
G.W.C. Lee
Col. & A.D.C.

Secy of war

RECORD DIVISION

Courtesy of the National Archives

Richmond Ap. 28d 1863

His Excellency
President Davis

The undersigned, members of Congress from North Carolina respectfully present the name of Colonel Edward D. Hall in command of the 46th North Carolina Regiment and recommend his promotion for gallant conduct and personal merit to the rank of Brigadier General. Col Hall has been in the service since the beginning of the war, has participated in many battles, and acquitted himself well in them all

Most respectfully
Thos D McDowell
Geo Davis
W. N. H. Smith
R R Bridgers
J. R. McLean
Tho: S. Ashe
A. H. Arrington
O. R. Kenan

State of North-Carolina,
EXECUTIVE DEPARTMENT,
Raleigh, 24 July 1863

Sir

I have learned with great pleasure that Col Edward D Hall has been recommended by many of his superior officers for promotion.

I would be doing injustice to Col Hall, if I did not add my testimony to his superior abilities as an officer, as well as his qualifications as a gentleman. His claims for promotion are equal to those of any officer from North Carolina – His services in the field and his devotion to the Cause, from the beginning of this Revolution, entitle him in my estimation to be ranked amongst those whose claims to promotion, should be first considered –

The promotion of Col Hall would not only be acceptable to the people of North Carolina but particularly gratifying to the Executive and I therefore recommend it without any hesitation – I am

Courtesy of the National Archives

Henry T. Clark ✓
WD 1893
Tarboro' N.C. Sept: 12, 1863

Brigadier Generals

Encloses letter, recommending Col: F. M. Parker 30th N.C. Regt: & Col: Edwd Hall 46th N.C. Regt: for the first vacancies among the Brigades of N.C. troops - mentions Cols: Ruffin & Leventhorpe as worthy of promotion. speaks of the characters of the first named officers - thinks that Genl Iverson should if possible be transferred to a Geo: Brigade and gives reasons therefor & expresses friendly sentiments &c. &c. -

✓ (~~two~~ enclosure)

~~Ack. [illegible]~~

~~[illegible]~~

~~[illegible] Brigade He had~~

~~[illegible]~~

~~[illegible]~~

~~[illegible] N. C. Brigade [illegible]~~

Refer enclosures to Secty of War for attention.

recd Sept: 16. J. D.

Courtesy of the National Archives

To the President

Col. Ed. Hall. 46th No Ca Regt. is regarded in this State as ~~one~~ one of the best officers in her Service. He had previous to the war exhibited his talents for military command by training and commanding of the best Volunteer Co in the State. — He went promptly into service in command of a Company with the 2. No Ca Regt. ~~from which he was soon promoted~~ to Major of 7th N.C.T. Stationed in Eastern No Carolina where he was for some time with a portion of his Regt and other detached Cos placed in a separate command and displayed admirable qualities for a superior officer and an independent command — But he was soon after made Colonel of 46th N.C. Regt. where his valuable services are well known to the authorities at Richmond. — Col Hall was Sheriff of his County before the war having the highest confidence of the community in his steady business habits. No officer in the army stands higher at home than Col Hall and his promotion I think would be most acceptable

Most Respectfully Submitted by
Henry T. Clark
Tarboro N.C.

Courtesy of the National Archives

Wilmington No Ca
Decr 29th 1863

Sir

Having been elected High Sheriff of New Hanover County I hereby respectfully tender my resignation as Colonel of the 46th Regt No Ca Troops of Coast Brigade

I have the honour to be
Respectfully
E D Hall
Col 46th No Car

Courtesy of the National Archives

State of North Carolina
New Hanover County Court Decr Term 1863
I Saml R Bunting Clerk of the Court of
Pleas and Quarter Sessions for the County
aforesaid do hereby certify that E. D.
Hall was duly elected Sheriff of
New Hanover County on the 15th day
of December 1863. by a majority of
the Justices of New Hanover County
present at Court.

In witness whereof I have hereunto
set my hand and affixed the seal
of said Court at office this 29
th day of December 1863

Saml R Bunting Clerk

Courtesy of the National Archives

Courtesy of the National Archives

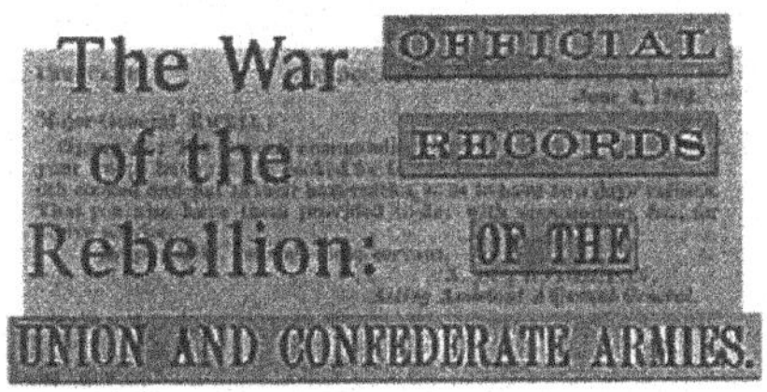

Records Related to Augusta County Regiments

Official Records : Documents Authored By Cooper, Samuel

June 19, 1861. From: S. COOPER, Adjutant and Inspector Gen. ,

Confederate Adjutant General Samuel Cooper writes Joseph E. Johnston concerning reinforcements and the strategic situation in June, 1861. Cooper refers to the benefit the Union would receive from advancing up the Valley as far as Staunton, thereby cutting important lines of communication.

July 17, 1861. From: S. COOPER, Adjutant and Inspector Gen. ,

In mid-July, 1861, Confederate General P. G. T. Beauregard faced a Federal advance on his positions around Manassas, VA. Staunton, VA, served as an important communications center as evidenced by Adjutant General Samuel Cooper's orders instructing Beauregard to get in touch with General Joseph Johnston through Staunton to inform him of the situation.

July 17, 1861. From: S. COOPER, Adjutant and Inspector Gen. ,

In mid-July, 1861, Confederate forces under Robert Garnett met defeat at the hands of George B. McClellan's Federals in what is now West Virginia. In this letter, Confederate Adjutant General Samuel Cooper orders General John B. Floyd to move to contain the damage. Staunton is mentioned as a possible defensive position.

July 18, 1861. From: S. COOPER, Adjutant and Inspector Gen. ,

In mid-July, 1861, Federal troops under George B. McClellan defeated Confederates under Robert Garnett in what is now West Virginia. In this letter, Confederate Adjutant General Samuel Cooper orders Colonel Angus McDonald to Staunton to defend the Central Railroad against any advance by McClellan.

July 21, 1861. From: S. COOPER, Adjutant-Gen. ,

Courtesy of the generalcooper.com

www.vcdh.virginia.edu

GENERAL FOOTNOTES

Chapter I-XII.

1. Jones, William; Southern Historical Society Papers, Vol III (January-June 1877), Richmond, VA; Pages 269-274 (also see www.generalcooper.com)

2. Association Secretary, Annual Reunion of the Association of the Graduates of the United States Military Academy; A.S. Barnes Co., NY: 1877.

3. Register of Graduates of the United State Military Academy (March 1802-January 1890); West Point, NY: 1890.

4. Cooper, Samuel; Internet www.generalcooper.com dated 2010.

5. Davis, Jefferson; 1-2 Volumes; The Rise and Fall of the Confederate Government; D. Appleton & Co., NY: 1881.

6. Cooper III, George Alexander; Compiled: A Short Sketch of his Grandfather General S. Cooper on the internet; undated.

7. Lee, Fitzhugh; A Sketch of the Late General S. Cooper on the internet: Undated.

8. Cooper, Samuel; Concise System of Instruction and Regulations for the Militia and Volunteers of the United States (Also known as Cooper's Tactic's 1852); United States Army, Washington, DC: 1836.

9. Dawson, E. Rowland; The Dawson Research Papers pertaining his great-grandfather The Late General S. Cooper; Southern Historical Society Collection, Vol III, Richmond, VA: 1877.

10. Jones, J. B.; A Rebel War Clerk's Diary 1810-1866; J.B. Lippincott & Co., Philadelphia, PA: 1866 (Reprinted Time-Life Books Inc., New York, NY: 1982).

11. Kean, COL Robert G.H.; ed. Younger, E.; Inside the Confederate Government (A Dairy); Oxford University Press, New York, NY: 1957

12. Corsan, W.C.; ed. Trask, B.H.; Two Months in the Confederate States; the Louisiana State University Press, Baton Rough, LA: 1996.

13. Trash, Benjamin H. ed. Corsan, W. C.; Two Months in the Confederate States; Louisiana State University Press, Baton Rough, LA: 1996.

14. Bush, Bryan S.; the Civil War of the Western Theater; Turner Publishing Co., Paducah, KY: 1998.

15. Coffman, Edward M.; the Regulars (the American Army 1898-1941); Harvard U. Belknap Press, Cambridge, MA: 2004.

16. Complied Service Records of Confederate Soldiers Who Served in Organizations from the Confederate/Rebel Archives; National Archives Microfilm Pubs, Microcopy; National Archives and Records Service, GSA; Washington, DC: 1959.

17. Confederate Hand-Book (A Compilation of Materials relating to the War between the States, 1861-1865); United Daughters of the Confederacy, Richmond, VA; Undated.

18. Confederate Military History; 1-12 Volumes; Confederate Publishing Co., Atlanta, GA: 1899.

19. Cooper, General Samuel; Rank Insignia & Uniforms of the Confederate States of America; Adjutant & Inspector General's Office, Richmond, VA, CSA: 1861.

20. Hardee, William J; Rifle and Light Infantry Tactics; United States Army, Washington, DC: 1855.

21. Harper & Brothers; the Civil War (A Pictorial History); the Fairfax Press, New York, NY: 1866.

22. Hewett, Janet B., et. al., eds.; Supplement to the Official Records of the Union and Confederate Armies; Broadfoot Publishing Co., Wilmington, NC: 1994.

23. Matthews, W. M.; "Letter from Camp Boone, 2nd Kentucky Infantry," John Kelly Ross Jr. Collection; Public Library, Paducah, KY: September 5, 1861.

24. Henderson, H.A.M.; "A Letter from Camp Boone," Louisville Daily Courier, 20 August 1861.

25. Office's of the Adjutant General, 13 Confederate States; Register of Commissions; 1861-1865.

26. Report of the Adjutant General of the State of Kentucky (Vol. 1 & 2 Confederate), Frankfort, KY: 1861-1865.

27. Sifakis, Stewart; Compendium of the Confederate Armies; Facts on File, Inc.; New York, NY: 1995.

28. The War of the Rebellion: A Compilation of the Official Records of the Union and Confederate Armies (Volumes I-IV); National Archives, Government Printing Office, Washington, DC: 1900.

29. Cooper, Samuel. Confederate States Army Regulations Handbook; Adjutant General's Office, Richmond, VA 1861-1864

30. Hall, COL Charles W.L.; Books to Bullets: A History of the 46th Regiment North Carolina Infantry; The Confederate Press, Jackson, MS: 2006.

31. Hall, COL Charles W.L.; Plowshares to Bayonets: A History of the 27th Regiment Mississippi Infantry; The Confederate Press, Jackson, MS: 2008

32. Hall, COL Charles W.L.; Revivals to Revolvers: A History of the 2nd Regiment Kentucky Infantry; The Confederate Press, Jackson, MS: 2010

33. Reeder, COL Red; the Southern Generals; Duell, Sloan and Pearce, New York, NY: 1965.

34. Warner, Ezra J.; General's in Gray, Louisiana State University Press, Baton Rough, LA: 1987.

35. Taylor, Walter H.; Four Years with General Lee (Ed, Robertson, J.I.); Civil War Centennial Series; Indiana University Press, Bloomington, IN: 1962.

36. Tower, R. Lockwood ed.; Lee's Adjutant (The Wartime Letters of COL Walter Herron Taylor 1862-1865); University of South Carolina Press, Columbia, SC: 1995

37. Cozzens, Peter; This Terrible Sound: the Battle of Chickamauga; University of Illinois Press, Chicago, IL: 1992.

38. Prushankin, Jeffery S.; A Crisis in Confederate Command; Louisiana State U. Press, Baton Rough, LA: 2005.

39. Woodworth, Steve E.; Jefferson Davis and His Generals (The Failure of Confederate Command in the West); University Press of Kansas, KS: 1987.

40. Lee, Richard M.; General Lee's City (Illustrated Guide to the Historical Sites of Confederate Richmond); EPM Publications Inc., McLean, VA: 1987.

41. Hattaway, Herman; General Stephen D. Lee; U. Mississippi Press—Kingsport Press, Kingsport, TN: 1976.

42. Sorrel, Gen, G. Moxley; Recollections of a Confederate Staff Officer; Morningside Bookstore Press, Dayton, OH: 1978.

43. Dabney, V.; The Last Review; Algonquin Books, Richmond, VA; 1932.

44. General Orders [microfilm]. Confederate States of America, Adjutant & Inspector General's Office, Richmond, VA: 1862-1865.

BIBLIOGRAPHY

A

Anderson, Ephraim M.; Memoirs: Historical and Personal (Companies of the First Missouri Confederate Brigade); Times Printing Co., St. Louis, MO: 1866 (Reprinted by Morningside Bookshop Press, Dayton, OH)

Association Secretary; Annual Reunion of the Association of the Graduates of the United States Military Academy; A.S. Barnes Co., NY: 1877.

B

Bearass, Edwin C. et. als; The Siege of Jackson (July 10-17, 1863); Gateway Press Inc., Baltimore, MD: 1981.

Boatner, Mark M.; The Civil War Dictionary; David McKay Co. Inc. (Van Press), New York, NY: 1959.

Botkin, B. A. ed.; A Civil War Treasury of Tales, Legends and Folklore; Promontory Press, New York, NY: 1960.

Brown, D. A.; The Bold Cavaliers (Morgan's 2nd Kentucky Cavalry Raiders); J. B. Lippincott Co., New York, NY: 1959.

Bush, Bryan S.; The Civil War of the Western Theater; Turner Publishing Co., Paducah, KY: 1998.

C

Coffman, Edward M.; the Regulars (the American Army 1898-1941); Harvard U. Belknap Press, Cambridge, MA: 2004.

Complied Service Records of Confederate Soldiers Who Served in Organizations from the Confederate/Rebel Archives; National Archives Microfilm Pubs, Microcopy; National Archives and Records Service, GSA; Washington, DC: 1959.

Confederate Hand-Book (A Compilation of Materials relating to the War between the States, 1861-1865); United Daughters of the Confederacy, Richmond, VA; Undated.

Confederate Military History; 1-12 Volumes; Confederate Publishing Co., Atlanta, GA: 1899.

Confederate Veteran. General Samuel Cooper, Vol XIV Issue 2, February 1906.

Confederate Veteran. Battle Flags of the Orphan Brigade, Vol. 32 Issue 6, June 1924 and Vol. 33 Issue 10, October 1925.

Confederate Veteran. Hoffman, John. The Confederate Collapse at the Battle of Missionary Ridge: The Report of James Patton Anderson and his brigade commanders. Dayton, OH: 1985.

Connelly, Thomas L.; Army of the Heartland; Louisiana State U. Press, Baton Rough, LA: 1967.

Cooper III, George Alexander; Compiled: A Short Sketch of his Grandfather General S. Cooper on the internet www.generalcooper.com ; Undated.

Cooper, Samuel; Concise System of Instructions and Regulations for the Militia and Volunteers of the United States (Revised as Cooper's Tactics, 1852); United States Army; Washington, DC: 1836.

Cooper, Samuel; Confederate States Army Regulations Handbook; Adjutant Geberal's Office, Richmond, VA: 1861-1864

Cooper, Samuel; Internet www.generalcooper.com dated 2010.

Cooper, Samuel; Rank Insignia & Uniforms of the Confederate States of America; Adjutant & Inspector General's Office, Richmond, VA, CSA: 1861.

Corsan, W.C.; ed. Trask, B.H.; Two Months in the Confederate States; The Louisiana State University Press, Baton Rough, LA: 1996.

Cozzens, Peter; This Terrible Sound: the Battle of Chickamauga; University of Illinois Press, Chicago, IL: 1992.

Crute, Joseph H. Jr.; Units of the Confederate States Army; Derwent Books, Midlothian,VA: 1987.

D

Dabney,V.;The Last Review;Algonquin Books, Richmond,VA; 1932.

Davis, Jefferson; 1-2 Volumes; The Rise and Fall of the Confederacy; D. Appleton & Co., NY: 1881.

Dawson, E. Rowland; The Dawson Research Papers pertaining to his Great-grandfather General S. Cooper; Southern Historical Society Collection, Vol III, Richmond,VA: 1877 (Also on the internet www.generalcooper.com)

Duke, B. W.; A History of Morgan Cavalry (ed. C. F. Holland); Civil War Centennial Series; Indiana University Press, Bloomington, IN: 1960.

E

F

Flato, Charles;The Golden Book of the Civil War; Golden Press, NY: 1961.

Folsom Club Collection Military Units serving in the Civil War; Louisville, KY: Undated.

G

General Orders [microfilm]. Confederate States of America, Adjutant & Inspector General's Office, Richmond,VA: 1862-1865.

Greenwell, Dale; The Third Mississippi Regiment—C.S.A.; Lewis Printing Service; Pascagoula, MS: 1972.

H

Hall, COL Charles W.L.; Books to Bullets: A History of the 46th Regiment North Carolina Infantry; The Confederate Press, Jackson, MS: 2006.

Hall, COL Charles W.L.; Plowshares to Bayonets: A History of the 27th Regiment Mississippi Infantry; The Confederate Press, Jackson, MS: 2008

Hall, COL Charles W.L.; Revivals to Revolvers: A History of the 2nd Regiment Kentucky Infantry; The Confederate Press, Jackson, MS: 2010

Hattaway, Herman; General Stephen D. Lee; U. Mississippi Press—Kingsport Press, Kingsport, TN: 1976.

Harper & Brothers; the Civil War (A Pictorial History); the Fairfax Press, New York, NY: 1866.

Hardee, William J,; Rifle and Light Infantry Tactics; United States Army, Washington, DC: 1855.

Henderson, H.A.M.; "A Letter from Camp Boone," Louisville Daily Courier, 20 August 1861.

Hewett, Janet B., et. al., eds.; Supplement to the Official Records of the Union and Confederate Armies; Broadfoot Publishing Co., Wilmington, NC: 1994.

Hood, J. B.; Advance and Retreat (personal experiences), Civil War Centennial Series; Indiana U. Press, Bloomington, IN:

Horn, Stanley F.; The Army of Tennessee CSA (A Military History); Babb's and Merrill Publishing Co.; New York, NY: 1941.

Hughes, Nathaniel L.; Bentonville (The Final Battle), University of North Carolina Press, Chapel Hill, NC: 1966.

Hurst, Jack; Nathan Bedford Forrest (A Biography), Vintage Books, Random House Inc., New York, NY: 1993.

I

Illustrated Atlas of the Civil War, Time-Life Book; Alexandra, VA: 1996.

J

Jones, J. B.; A Rebel War Clerk's Diary 1810-1866; J.B. Lippincott & Co., Philadelphia, PA: 1866 (Reprinted Time-Life Books Inc., New York, NY:1982).

Jones, William; Southern Historical Society Papers, Vol III (January-June 1877); Richmond,VA; Pages 269-274 (Also see www.generalcooper.com)

Joyce, Fred;"Infantry to Cavalry," Southern Bivouac,Vol. 3, Part 3, February 6, 1885.

K

Kean, COL Robert G.H.; ed. Younger, E.; Inside the Confederate Government (A Dairy); Oxford University Press, New York, NY: 1957

"Kentuckians Going South," Louisville Daily Courier, July 11, 1861.

Kerby, Robert L.; Kirby Smith's Confederacy (the Trans-Mississippi); Columbia U. Press, New York, NY: 1972.

Kiwan, A. D. ed.; Johnny Green of the Orphan Brigade; University of Kentucky Press, Lexington, KY: 1984.

L

Lee, Fitzhugh; A Sketch of the Late General S. Cooper on the internet www.generalcooper.com : Undated.

Lee, Fitzhugh; Confederate Soldier in the Civil War; The Fairfax Press (Crown Publishers),VA: 1895.

Lee, Richard M.; General Lee's City (Illustrated Guide to the Historical Sites of Confederate Richmond); EPM Publications Inc., McLean,VA: 1987.

Lochiel, "Kentucky Brigade for the Confederate States' Service," Louisville Daily Courier, 16 July 1861.

M

Map of Montgomery County, Tennessee, ca. 1872; Tennessee State Library and Archives, Nashville, TN: 1872.

Marshall, John L.; "Col. Thomas W. Thompson," Southern Bivouac, Vol 1, No. 1, September 1882.

Matthews, W. M.; "Letter from Camp Boone, 2nd Kentucky Infantry," John Kelly Ross Jr. Collection; Public Library, Paducah, KY: September 5, 1861.

Miller, Francis T.; The Photographic History of the Civil War; Thomas Yoseloff, Inc. (Castle Books), New York, NY: 1957.

Mullen, Frank; "Letter from Frank Mullen, 2nd Kentucky Infantry." (Orphan Brigade Kinfolk Association), Camp Douglas, IL, October 16, 1863.

N

O

Office's of the Adjutant General, 13 Confederate States; Register of Commissions; 1861-1865.

P

Parrish, T. Michael; Taylor, Richard; U. North Carolina Press, Chapel Hill, NC: 1992

Payne, L. D. "Louis Douglas Payne's War Experience," unpublished: undated.

Register of Graduates of the United States Military Academy (March 1802-January 1890); West Point, NY: 1890

Prushankin, Jeffery S.; A Crisis in Confederate Command; Louisiana State U. Press, Baton Rough, LA: 2005.

Q

R

Ratchford, J. W.; Some Reminiscences of Persons and Incidents of the Civil War; Shoal Creek Publishers, Atlanta, GA: 1971.

Reeder, COL Red; the Southern Generals; Duell, Sloan and Pearce, New York, NY: 1965.

Rietti, J. C.; Military Annals of Mississippi Confederates; Reprint Co. Publishers, Spartanburg, SC: 1976.

Robertson Jr., James I. and Kunstler, Mort; The Confederate Spirit, Rutledge Hill Press, Nashville, TN: 2000.

Report of the Adjutant General of the State of Kentucky (Vol. 1 & 2 Confederate), Frankfort, KY: 1861-1865.

S

Sifakis, Stewart; Compendium of the Confederate Armies; Facts on File, Inc.; New York, NY: 1995.

Sheets, George W.; "Letter from Camp Boone," Louisville Daily Courier, 17 September 1861.

"Sketch of Life of Gen. W. T. Withers," undated clippings, Lexington Herald, Lexington, KY.

Sorrel, Gen, G. Moxley; Recollections of a Confederate Staff Officer; Morningside Bookstore Press, Dayton, OH: 1978.

Swiggett, Howard; The Rebel Raider (A Life of John Hunt Morgan); The Bobb's and Merrill Co. Publishers, Indianapolis, IN: 1934.

Sword, Wiley; Embrace an Angry Wind (The Confederacy's Last Hurrah); The General's Books, Columbus, OH: 1994.

T

Taylor, Walter H.; Four Years with General Lee (ed, Robertson, J.I.); Civil War Centennial Series; Indiana University Press, Bloomington, IN: 1962.

The War of the Rebellion: A Compilation of the Official Records of the Union and Confederate Armies (Volumes I-IV); National Archives, Government Printing Office, Washington, DC: 1900.

Thompson, Ed. Porter; History of the Orphan Brigade; Louisville, KY: 1898.

Tower, R. Lockwood ed.; Lee's Adjutant (The Wartime Letters of COL Walter Herron Taylor 1862-1865); University of South Carolina Press, Columbia, SC: 1995

Trash, Benjamin H. ed. Corsan, W. C.; Two Months in the Confederate States; Louisiana State University Press, Baton Rough, LA: 1996.

Tucker, Glenn; Chickamauga: Bloody Battles of the West, Morningside Press, Columbus, OH: 1976.

U

V

W

W., J. L.; "Letter from Camp near Bowling Green," Louisville Daily Courier, December 6, 1861.

Walden, Geoffrey R.; "Opposing Sherman's March to the Sea;" 1995 (Researching your Orphan Brigade Ancestors, Ancestry).

Walden, Geoff; "The Orphan Brigade as Mounted Infantry Campaign in South Carolina, April 1865;" (Researching your Orphan Brigade Ancestors, Ancestry).

Walden, Geoff; "Surrender of the Orphan Brigade (The Blackest Day of Our Lives);" (Researching your Orphan Brigade Ancestors, Ancestry).

War of the Rebellion: Official Records of the Union and Confederate Armies. Published by the War Department, Washington, D.C.: 1881-1900.

Warner, Ezra J.; General's in Gray, Louisiana State University Press, Baton Rough, LA: 1987.

Wiley, Bell I.; The Embattled Confederates, Harper & Roe Company, New York, NY: 1964.

Woodworth, Steve E.; Jefferson Davis and His Generals (The Failure of Confederate Command in the West); University Press of Kansas, KS: 1987.

Woodworth, Steven E. and Winkle, Kenneth J.; Foreword by McPherson, James M.; Atlas of the Civil War, Oxford University Press, New York, NY: 2004.

X

Y

Younger, Edward ed.; Inside the Confederate Government (The Dairy of Robert Garlick Hill Kean, Head of the Bureau of War); Oxford University Press, New York, NY: 1957.

Z

THE RAILROADS OF THE CONFEDERATE STATES, 1861

1. Baltimore & Ohio
2. Alexandria, Loudoun & Hampshire
3. Orange & Alexandria
4. Winchester & Potomac
5. Virginia Central
6. Richmond, Fredericksburg & Potomac
7. Richmond & York River
8. Richmond & Petersburg
9. Richmond & Danville
10. South Side
11. Norfolk & Petersburg
12. Petersburg R. R.
13. Seaboard & Roanoke
14. Virginia & Tennessee
15. Piedmont R. R.
16. Raleigh & Gaston
17. Roanoke Valley
18. Wilmington & Weldon
19. Atlantic & North Carolina
20. North Carolina
21. Western North Carolina
22. Western R. R.
23. Atlantic, Tennessee & Ohio
24. Wilmington, Charlotte & Rutherford
25. Wilmington & Manchester
26. Cheraw & Darlington
27. Charlotte & South Carolina
28. King's Mountain
29. South Carolina R. R.
30. Greenville & Columbia
31. Spartanburg & Union
32. Laurens R. R.
33. Blue Ridge R. R.
34. Northeastern
35. Charleston & Savannah
36. Georgia R. R.
37. Augusta & Milledgeville
38. Western & Atlantic
39. Etowah R. R.
40. Rome R. R.
41. Central R. R. of Georgia
42. Macon & Western
43. Upson County
44. Macon & Brunswick
45. Southwestern R. R.
46. Muscogee R. R.
47. Augusta & Savannah
48. Savannah, Albany & Gulf
49. Atlantic & Gulf
50. Brunswick & Florida
51. Atlanta & West Point
52. Florida, Atlantic & Gulf Central
53. Florida R. R.
54. Pensacola & Georgia
55. Tallahassee R. R.
56. Alabama & Florida R. R. of Fla.
57. Alabama & Florida R. R. of Ala.
58. Montgomery & Eufaula
59. Montgomery & West Point
60. Tuskegee R. R.
61. Mobile & Girard
62. Mobile & Great Northern
63. Spring Hill R. R.
64. Mobile & Ohio
65. Mississippi, Gainesville & Tuscaloosa
66. Memphis & Charleston
67. Wills Valley
68. Nashville & Chattanooga
69. Winchester & Alabama
70. McMinnville & Manchester
71. Tennessee & Alabama
72. Nashville & Northwestern
73. Louisville & Nashville
74. Memphis, Clarksville & Louisville
75. Edgefield & Kentucky
76. East Tennessee & Georgia
77. East Tennessee & Virginia
78. Knoxville & Kentucky
79. Rogersville & Jefferson
80. Memphis & Ohio
81. Northeast & Southwest
82. Alabama & Mississippi Rivers
83. Cahaba, Marion & Greensboro
84. New Orleans & Ohio
85. Mississippi Central
86. Mississippi & Tennessee
87. Memphis & Little Rock
88. New Orleans, Jackson & Great Northern
89. Southern R. R. of Mississippi
90. Raymond R. R.
91. Jefferson & Lake Pontchartrain
92. Pontchartrain R. R.
93. Mexican Gulf R. R.
94. New Orleans, Opelousas & Great Western
95. West Feliciana R. R.
96. Clinton & Port Hudson
97. Baton Rouge, Grosse Tete & Opelousas
98. Vicksburg, Shreveport & Texas
99. Alexandria & Cheneyville
100. Texas & New Orleans
101. Eastern Texas R. R.
102. Buffalo Bayou, Brazos & Colorado
103. Houston Tap & Brazoria
104. Galveston, Houston & Henderson
105. Houston & Texas Central
106. Washington County R. R.
107. San Antonio & Mexican Gulf
108. Memphis, El Paso & Pacific
109. Southern Pacific
110. Manassas Gap
111. Alabama & Tennessee Rivers
112. Hungary Branch
113. Grand Gulf & Port Gibson

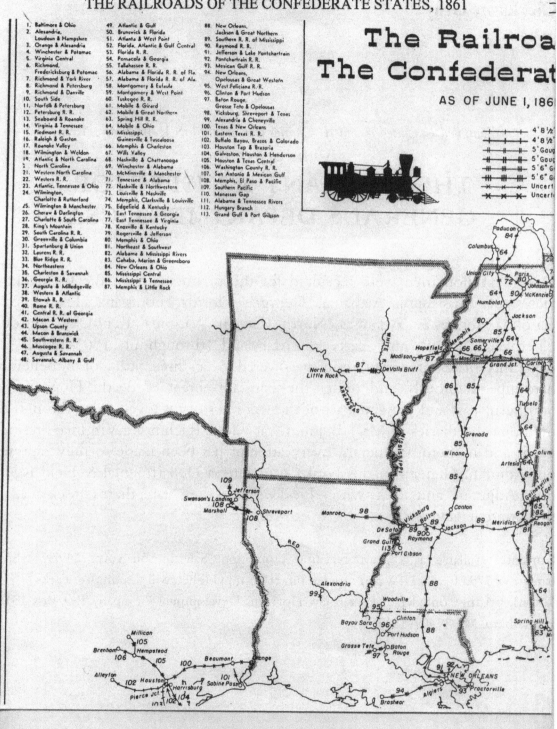

The Railroa
The Confederat

AS OF JUNE 1, 186

4'8½"
4'8½"
5' Gaug
5' Gaug
5'6" G
5'6" G
Uncert
Uncert

Paducah
Columbus
Union City
Paris
Johnsonville
McKenzie
Humboldt
Jackson
Memphis
Hopefield
Somerville
Madison
Moscow
Grand Jct.
Corinth
North Little Rock
DeValls Bluff
WHITE R.
ARKANSAS R.
MISSISSIPPI R.
Tupelo
Grenada
Winona
Artesia
Jefferson
Swanson's Landing
Marshall
Shreveport
Monroe
Vicksburg
Bolton
Canton
Jackson
Meridian
DeSoto
Raymond
Grand Gulf
Port Gibson
RED R.
Alexandria
Woodville
Bayou Sara
Clinton
Port Hudson
Grosse Tete
Baton Rouge
Spring Hill
Millican
Brenham
Hempstead
Beaumont
Orange
Alleyton
Houston
Harrisburg
Pierce Jct.
Sabine Pass
NEW ORLEANS
Algiers
Proctorville
Brashear

"COOPER'S ADJUTANTS" CSA
____________"Limited Edition"_______________
★ ★ ★ PRE-PUBLICATION ORDER FORM ★ ★ ★
Send to: ____________________________ Ship by:
Address: ____________________________USPS_
City/State/Zip: ______________________UPS_
Tel #: _____________ Email: ___________Other_
Payment Type: Check__ or Money Order__
Make Payable: COL Charles W.L. Hall

"COOPER'S ADJUTANTS" CSA
____________"Limited Edition"_______________

★ ★ ★ PRE-PUBLICATION ORDER FORM ★ ★ ★
Send to: ____________________________ Ship by:
Address: ____________________________USPS_
City/State/Zip: ______________________UPS_
Tel #: _____________ Email: ___________Other_
Payment Type: Check__ or Money Order__
Make Payable: COL Charles W.L. Hall

"COOPER'S ADJUTANTS" CSA
____________"Limited Edition"_______________

★ ★ ★ PRE-PUBLICATION ORDER FORM ★ ★ ★
Send to: ____________________________ Ship by:
Address: ____________________________USPS_
City/State/Zip: ______________________UPS_
Tel #: _____________ Email: ___________Other_
Payment Type: Check__ or Money Order__
Make Payable: COL Charles W.L. Hall

____

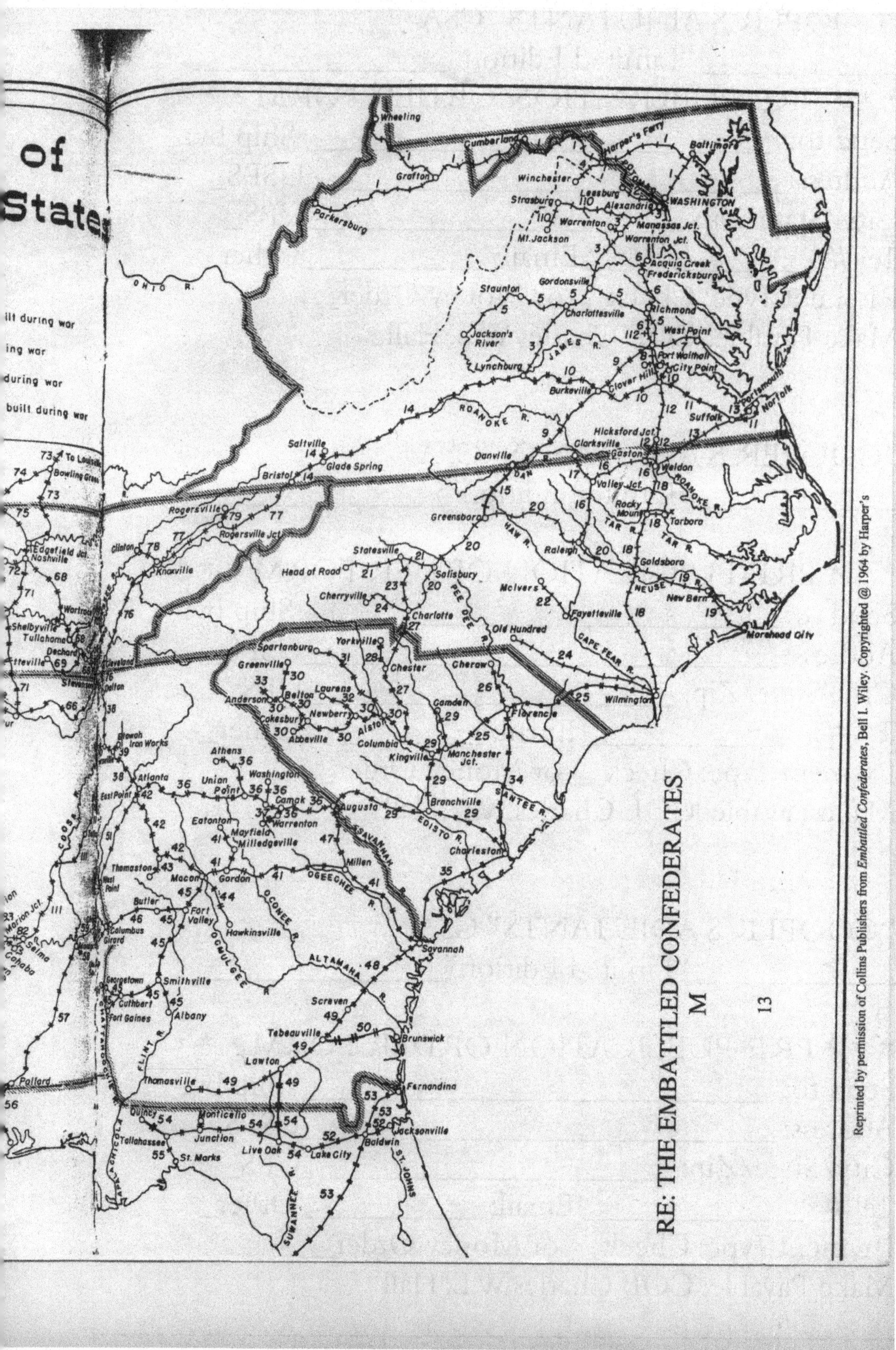

RE: THE EMBATTLED CONFEDERATES

M

13